Marriage: It's a God Thing

Marriage
IT'S A *God* THING

WILLIAM P. ROBERTS

Franciscan
MEDIA
Cincinnati, Ohio

For my wife Challon
with much love
and many thanks
for the wonderful journey

All quotations from the documents of the Second Vatican Council are taken from Austin
Flannery, O.P., General Editor, *Vatican Council II* (Northport, N.Y.: Costello, 1996).
Unless otherwise specified, Scripture passages have been taken from the *New Revised
Standard Version Bible,* copyright ©1989 by the Division of Christian Education of the
National Council of the Churches of Christ in the U.S.A., and used by permission.
All rights reserved.
NJB after a biblical quotation refers to *The New Jerusalem Bible*
(Garden City, N.Y.: Doubleday, 1985).
NAB after a biblical quotation refers to *The New American Bible*
(New York: Catholic Book Publishing, 1992).

Cover and book design by Mark Sullivan
Cover photo ©istockphoto.com / Iryna Shpulak

LIBRARY OF CONGRESS CATALOGING-IN-PUBLICATION DATA

Roberts, William P., 1931-
Marriage : it's a God thing / William P. Roberts.
p. cm.
ISBN 978-0-86716-747-4 (pbk. : alk. paper) 1. Marriage—Religious aspects—
Catholic Church. I. Title.

BX2250.R633 2007
248.4'82—dc22

2006037880

ISBN 978-0-86716-747-4

Published by Franciscan Media
28 W. Liberty Street
Cincinnati, OH 45202
www.FranciscanMedia.org

Printed in the United States of America.

.contents.

Foreword .... *ix*

Part One: A Marriage Transformed by Christ 1
   Introduction 3
   Chapter One: Christ: The Human Face of God 7
   Chapter Two: Trinitarian Presence 21
   Chapter Three: The Word Enfleshed 33
   Chapter Four: The Primacy of Love 45
   Chapter Five: Authority Inverted 53
   Chapter Six: Suffering and Death Transformed 61
   Chapter Seven: Earthly Marriage and the Eternal
                  Wedding Feast 69

Part Two: Marriage as a Unique Vocation 75
   Introduction 77
   Chapter Eight: Be Open to the Spirit 79
   Chapter Nine: Pursue the Fullness of Holiness 89
   Chapter Ten: Participate in the Mission of Christ 97
   Chapter Eleven: Some Liturgical Implications 109

Part Three: Marriage: A Life of Prayer 115
   Introduction 117
   Chapter Twelve: Prayer: A Living Response to God 119
   Chapter Thirteen: Praying in Countless Ways 133

Epilogue 147

Notes 150

Index 157

Scripture Index 161

The Catholic tradition holds that marriage is one of the seven sacraments. Up until the last few decades, however, this truth was usually understood in terms of the natural, human reality of marriage being "raised" by Christ to the "level" of a sacrament. This sacrament took place at the wedding ceremony in the church. Further, even though the Latin tradition of the Roman Catholic church teaches that the couple themselves are the ministers of this sacrament, much of the common mindset is reflected in the often-heard expression, "Father So-and-So married us." The impression given in the past was that the sacrament of marriage was something the couple "received" to give them the grace to weather the trials and challenges of marriage, and to live their marriage according to God's commandments and the laws of the church.

Combined with this mentality was the view that if one truly wanted to pursue a life of holiness, one entered the priesthood or religious life. Marriage was generally considered a path for those who were not stalwart enough to embrace either of those vocations.

Since the Second Vatican Council, a much richer understanding of the meaning of Christian marriage as a sacrament has evolved. This book takes some of these important insights and, in concrete, practical ways, tries to show how they can make a difference in the day-to-day lives of every couple striving for a happier, more fulfilling and holier marriage.

This approach is built on three basic insights:

First, marriage is not something that took place only in the past. It is a journey that the couple embarked on at the wedding ceremony, but what it becomes and where it goes depends on the choices they make throughout the duration of the marriage. The marital journey is continually being created. A couple can become either more married or less married depending on how they decide to treat each other on a daily basis.

Second, a couple grows in their marriage as a sacrament to the degree that they experience it as a visible sign of Christ's enriching and transforming love for them and his intimate presence with them. This experience depends on the deepening quality of their relationship with Christ and with each other.

Third, marriage is a true vocation, a call from God. For Christians, this marital vocation is rooted in the baptismal call to live in Christ and to share his mission. Accordingly, a couple does not grow in holiness despite the "distractions" of marriage. Rather, they are empowered to find God and Christ in all the little details—joyful and bothersome—that constitute the realities of married life.

The purpose of this book is to help us reflect on the spirituality that flows from these insights, a spirituality that many are already living through marriage without, perhaps, ever having named it as such. Recognizing this spirituality will help us pursue it with greater awareness and deliberation.

The book is divided into three main sections. Part one relates Jesus' changing the water into wine at the marriage feast of Cana to show some of the many ways the presence of Christ can transform the "water" of our marital journey into "the best of wine." In part two we reflect on marriage as a true vocation, rooted in our baptismal call to be followers of Christ. Finally, since the spirituality of our marital journey depends on prayer, part three reflects on the meaning of prayer in the life of the couple. It probes how we can pray in the context of a busy (sometimes hectic) married life and how our marriage itself can become a living prayer.

Despite all the despair about the future of marriage and the family voiced so often today, this book is written with the hope that the more each of us lights the candle of a mutually loving, faith-filled marriage, the grace of God can shine through our light and conquer the darkness that plagues our world in so many ways.

William P. Roberts
Dayton, Ohio
Easter Sunday, 2006

A Marriage Transformed by Christ

*T*o say that marriage is a sacrament, an effective sign of Christ's grace-giving presence and love, is to believe that the reality of marriage has been profoundly enriched because of the Christ event. The first part of this book explores some of the concrete ways in which our openness to Christ in faith and love can make a real difference in the mutual fruitfulness and happiness we hope to achieve in our marriage.

A reflection on Jesus' miracle at the marriage feast of Cana provides a good context to consider Christ's radical transformation of the significance of marriage.

> On the third day there was a wedding at Cana in Galilee. The mother of Jesus was there, and Jesus and his disciples had also been invited. And they ran out of wine, since the wine provided for the feast had all been used, and the mother of Jesus said to him, "They have no wine." Jesus said, "Woman, what do you want from me? My hour has not come yet." His mother said to the servants,

Do whatever he tells you." There were six stone water jars standing there, meant for the ablutions that are customary among the Jews: each could hold twenty or thirty gallons. Jesus said to the servants, "Fill the jars with water," and they filled them to the brim. Then he said to them, "Draw some out now and take it to the president of the feast." They did this; the president tasted the water, and it had turned into wine. Having no idea where it came from—though the servants who had drawn the water knew—the president of the feast called the bridegroom and said, "Everyone serves good wine first and the worse wine when the guests are well wined; but you have kept the best wine till now." This was the first of Jesus' signs: It was at Cana in Galilee. He revealed his glory, and his disciples believed in him. (John 2:1–11, NJB)

Let us consider five of the details of this first sign that Jesus performed, as described in John's Gospel.

1. This sign is performed at a wedding feast.
2. Jesus has the six stone water jars filled with water. He does not create the wine out of the emptiness of the jars.
3. Each jar can hold twenty or thirty gallons. The servants fill all six of them to the brim. So we are talking about quite an abundance.
4. These are not any ordinary water jars. They are used for a specific purpose, namely for the ablutions that were customary for the Jews, according to the purification rites of the Old Law.
5. This water is transformed not just into any usual wine. It is changed into the best wine served at the wedding feast.

A sign is a visible reality that points to an invisible one. So, what is the invisible reality that is revealed in the details of this first sign performed by Jesus? Renowned Scripture scholar Raymond Brown, offers some insights.

The primary focus of this narrative, Brown insists, is on Jesus, "the one sent by the Father to bring salvation to the world. What shines through is *his glory*, and the only reaction that is emphasized is the *belief* of the disciples."[1]

Brown then addresses the question of how Jesus' changing the water into wine reveals his glory to his disciples. The evangelist intends "to call attention to the replacement of the water prescribed for Jewish purification by the choicest of wines. This replacement is a sign of who Jesus is, namely, the one sent by the Father who is now the only way to the Father. All previous religious institutions, customs and feasts lose meaning in his presence."

Brown goes on to point out that some of the symbols in the Cana narrative appear elsewhere in the Scriptures. The changing of the water into wine is set in the context of a wedding. In Isaiah (54:4–8 and 62:4–5) the wedding is used to symbolize the messianic days.

The water is replaced by choice wine, better than what the guests had been thus far drinking. In the synoptic tradition, seemingly in the context of a wedding feast (Mark 2:19), we find Jesus using the symbolism of new wine in old wineskins in order to compare his new teaching with the customs of the Pharisees. (Note that this incident occurs at the beginning of the Synoptic account of the ministry just as Cana is at the beginning of the Johannine account.) Thus the head-waiter's statement at the end of the scene, "You have kept the choice wine until now," can be understood as the proclamation of the coming of the messianic days.

The abundance of wine, which Brown calculates at 120 gallons, also symbolizes the messianic era. "One of the consistent OT [Old Testament] figures for the joy of the final days is an abundance of wine (Amos ix 13–14; Hos xiv 7; Jer xxxi 12)." I particularly like the imagery in the reference to Amos: "the mountains will run with new wine and the hills all flow with it" (NJB).

In summary, Jesus' changing the water into wine symbolizes his transformation of the old dispensation of salvation into the new. He is the fulfillment of the messianic promises, and has brought to completion God's self-revelation. As the Letter to the Hebrews states, "Long ago God spoke to our ancestors in many and various ways by the prophets, but in these last days he has spoken to us by a Son, whom he appointed heir of all things, through whom he also created the worlds" (1:1–2).

In this part of the book I want to reflect on several of the concrete ways in which the Christ event has radically transformed our life of faith in general, and then to explore in particular the implications that each can have for the enrichment of Christian marriage.

chapter one

CHRIST: THE HUMAN FACE OF GOD

ne of the biggest struggles of faith for many people is the great divide between the divine and the human. We believe in God, and we can even apply certain words from our human vocabulary to describe God. But we are also keenly aware that any words we use draw very imperfect comparisons.

God, after all, is God—the infinite and eternal Spirit. We are embodied humans, so very finite, enduring on this earth but a brief, flashing moment. God is the ultimate foundation, the ultimate source, the support of all creation, of all life. We are contingent, dependent, vulnerable. So how do we get any grasp of this God who seems so infinitely distant?

It is the reality of Jesus and our God-given belief in him that has changed the water of our faith in a distant God into the wine of an intimate experience of God in the very person of Christ. For Christ is indeed Emmanuel, meaning, "God-is-with-us" (Matthew 1:23). He is the very Word of God in human flesh, who, in the words of John the Evangelist,

> lived among us, and we have seen his glory, the glory as of a father's only son, full of grace and truth. (John 1:14)

> No one has ever seen God. It is God the only Son, who is close to the Father's heart, who has made him known. (John 1:18)

> "Whoever has seen me," Jesus said to Philip, "has seen the Father." (John 14:9)

To see the face of Christ, therefore, is to see the face of God. While no one living today has seen the face of the mortal Jesus, we can picture his human form in our imagination. We have no idea what a risen body actually looks like, but we can image Jesus' risen, embodied self in ways we cannot even begin to imagine God. Our belief that this crucified and risen Christ is the Son, the Word of God who now sits at the right hand of the Father, enables us to see with the eyes of faith that he is totally with God, and God is totally with him.

Wherever and whenever this risen Jesus is with us, God is with us. To encounter Jesus and be graced by his presence is to be graced by the presence of God. To hear the word of Jesus is to hear the Word of God. To feel the healing touch of the hand of Jesus is to feel the healing touch of the "hand" of God. To experience in the depths of our being the empathy and compassion of Jesus is to experience the empathy and compassion of God. And that experience can be everywhere and always, for Jesus himself said, "I will not leave you orphaned; I am coming to you" (John 14:18). "And remember, I am with you always, to the end of the age" (Matthew 28:20).

To find God we need not look beyond the horizon or up to the distant skies. We need only gaze in prayerful contemplation into the face of the risen Christ who is with us in our mundane lives. It is this Christ who, in words attributed to Saint Patrick, is "Christ…with us, / Christ before us, Christ in us, / Christ over us."[1]

But where, we might ask, do we find the face of Christ? Saint Paul leads us to an answer when he proclaims that we are the body of Christ (1 Corinthians 12:12–30). In faith, we can see Christ in other people. And this can be nowhere more possible than in a loving, respectful and faith-filled Christian marriage where we give to one another the gift of ourselves. Christian marriage is, after all, a unique sacrament precisely because it can be, in a very special and intimate way, a sign of Christ's grace-filled presence and love.

Christ can transform the water of marriage into the best of wine, if we relate to each other in ways that manifest the presence of Christ. Our encounter with one another can be an encounter with Christ.

We can grow in this marital spirituality:

1. Through our presence. By being truly present to our spouses, we allow them to experience Christ's own grace-filled presence.
2. Through our words. Our words should contain, echo and reinforce Christ's words.
3. Through our touch. A gentle human touch can be healing and soothing. Christ's own healing powers often came through touching someone.
4. Through our compassion. In demonstrating mercy and tenderness, we offer our spouses the opportunity to feel Christ's compassion through our own.

PRESENCE

All sacraments are visible signs of invisible grace. In pre–Vatican II times, grace was often talked about as if it was a thing pumped into us to help us obey the laws of God and the church and to aid us in becoming more holy. Many of us from that era remember the milk bottles that Sister drew on the blackboard to illustrate how one grew in grace. The empty milk bottle showed the person with no grace. The partly filled milk bottles stood for persons with varying degrees of grace. The filled milk bottle signified someone like Mary, who is full of grace.

Contemporary theology reminds us that grace is not a quantity. Grace is God's outpouring of self to us in love and friendship. This reality is referred to as uncreated grace. If we are open to God, then under the impact of God's self-gift we are personally transformed. This transformation in us is created grace.

In Christian faith God's most visible manifestation of his self-gift to us is in sending his Word, his Son to be one among us. "For God so loved the world that he gave his only Son, so that everyone who believes in him may not perish but may have eternal life" (John 3:16).

Jesus spent himself in his public ministry sharing in personal ways the gift of himself with others: in his teaching, his conversing with them and his sharing meals with them. He let the power within him flow out to heal the sick, drive out evil spirits, raise the dead to life and bring us to more intimate union with God.

He was faithful to his ministry to us even when it cost him his life. In his tortuous death he continued to give of himself. "Father, forgive them; for they do not know what they are doing" (Luke 23:34). "Father, into your hands I commend my spirit" (Luke 23:46). In John's description of Jesus' death, Jesus bowed his head and "gave up his spirit" (19:30).[2]

In the Gospels, the risen Christ is depicted as continuing to give of himself in grace-giving ways. This is vividly brought out in Jesus' Easter evening appearance to his disciples. Though the doors of the house were locked, Jesus stood among them and said, "Peace be with you." Then he breathed on them and said, "Receive the Holy Spirit" (John 20:19–23).

Christ continues to communicate the gift of himself to us in grace-giving, life-giving ways. He does this most visibly in the sacraments. In marriage he graces us in and through our gracious, graceful and grace-filled present (presence) of ourselves to each other, but the transforming effect of Christ's presence in our marriage depends on the quality and effectiveness of that self-giving presence.

This presence demands much more than just being there physically. It involves being aware of others and being interested in who they are and what they are about. It's listening to their inner being and responding from the depths of your own care and concern. This kind of presence, perhaps more than anything else, determines the difference between a happy, satisfying marital relationship and one that leaves the other very much alone.

"I love my husband," Sara tearfully told me as she sat in my office years ago, distraught and confused. "He is a good man, He works hard and provides for my material needs. His job takes him away a great deal, but I can cope with that. My real problem is that when he is here he is only physically present. He never enters into my world. He is oblivious to what is going on inside me emotionally and spiritually. He never expresses warmth and affection. I consider him an emotional zero. I feel empty and alone. After three years of marriage I just can't put up with this any more."

Sara, indeed, is not alone in this kind of complaint. Her discontent highlights the central importance of personal presence as an essential element in an enriching marriage. It is also an integral part of a spirituality of marriage. And this for three reasons:

First, being personally present takes a lot of virtue. We have to be unselfish, willing to go out of ourselves and expend the energy necessary to reach into the deeper levels of the other's being. We have to be generous enough to listen and be open to our spouses and allow them to penetrate into the deeper dimensions of our being. We have to be concerned enough about the inner growth of the other as well as ourselves to make this a significant priority in our relationship.

Second, the personal presence of a spouse addresses some of the deepest longings in us—desires that physical things can never fully satisfy. We yearn to love and be loved. We long for deep companionship with someone. If our spouse is incapable or unwilling to address that longing, the marriage can become intolerable. As a wise person once said, it can be hard to live alone when you are living alone, but far more painful to live alone when you are not living alone.

Third, somehow, consciously or unconsciously, we touch and are touched by God when we are in touch with the spirit (the depth of being) of the other. As Augustine said, we cannot rest until we rest in God. Only in the afterlife do we see God face to face. In this life, God's presence is communicated to us in a special way through our intimate spousal presence to one another. The Spirit of God's presence is manifest in our spiritual presence to each other.

WORDS

Jesus Christ is the Word of God. He came on earth to speak his Word about God, about himself, about us. The Risen Christ continues to communicate his Word to us through the Scriptures and through the community of believers. He will always be true to his Word, the Word of his New Covenant with us. And his Word gives life, for "eternal life is this: / to know you, / the only true God, and Jesus Christ whom you have sent" (John 17:3, NJB).

There are many ways in which we can allow the Word who is Christ to transform our marriage. The first is occasionally and briefly to focus alone or together in silent waiting and allow Christ as God's Word to communicate to us right now. What is he saying to us? Where is he leading us?

We can read and share together favorite Scripture passages, especially from the Gospels. One way of doing this is first to reflect briefly on God speaking to us through this particular text. Then read the passage out loud. Pause for a brief reflection. Then discuss what meaning this text might have for your married life right now. This could be done in a few minutes. If you wish to make this a daily practice, it might be good to choose a regular time.

If you are not sure where to begin in the Scriptures, perhaps the dozens of Scripture references and quotations throughout this book could serve as a start.

We can share often and as deeply as we can our word with each other: the word of who God is for us; the word of who we are for one another. It is important to express countless times a day our words of love and appreciation for one another. We need to hear each other affirm, support and encourage us. This creates a constructive atmosphere that makes us more receptive to the words of correction and criticism that are also necessary and inevitable as we strive to lead ourselves to greater growth as human beings and marriage partners.

Several students over the years have revealed in class that they have never heard their parents tell each other "I love you." One of these students came to me later and added: "I confronted my parents on this once and their reply was, 'Oh, we know we love each other; we don't have to say it.'" Well, there is a saying that I read once that goes something like: Being grateful or loving someone and not saying it is like winking at someone in the dark; you may know it, but the other doesn't. Of course one might say actions speak louder than words. True, but words are essential to affirm and explain what lies behind the action. No one is a mind reader. What we are thinking must be expressed in words.

To reveal the fullness of God to us, God "spoke" the Word into human flesh. God continues to speak this Word through Christ and through our words. Marital intimacy depends on how well we allow Christ to do this.

T o u c h

God has touched the human race in a most visible, tangible way by sending his Son, our healer, our redeemer, our savior into the midst of our sin-torn humanity. God has, as it were, reached down into the heart of the human scene and affected it from within through the humanity of Jesus Christ. In Christ, the Divine has met and forever touched humanity at its roots.

A brief perusal of the Gospels reveals many occasions in which the healing power of Jesus was communicated through his human touch. The saving power of his Spirit was transmitted through his physical touch of another's body, bringing about diverse kinds of healings.

A touch can cleanse and purify, as experienced by a man "covered with leprosy." He approached Jesus and fell prostrate before him, pleading, "Lord, if you choose, you can make me clean." Stretching out his hand, Jesus touched him and said, "I do choose. Be made clean." The man was immediately cleansed of his leprosy (see Luke 5:12–13).

A human touch can help an ill person feel better and help them return to their normal way of living. Peter's mother-in-law discovered this when she was lying in her bed with a fever. When Jesus touched her hand, the fever left her "and she got up and began to serve him" (Matthew 8:14–15).

A human touch can help us see in a new light. In John's Gospel, when Jesus cured the man born blind, "he spat on the ground and made mud with the saliva and smeared the mud on the man's eyes…". At Jesus' direction he washed in the pool of Siloam, "and came back able to see" (John 9:6–7).

Jesus' touching was not limited to miraculous events. People brought little children to Jesus, so he could touch them. Despite the disciples' opposition, Jesus embraced the children, "laid his hands on them, and blessed them" (Mark 10:13–16).

Jesus also permitted himself to be touched by others, as in the case of the woman who had endured for twelve years a hemorrhage that no one could cure. As soon as she touched the fringe of his cloak, power went out from him and the hemorrhage stopped (Luke 8:43–48). He welcomed the woman who was a sinner and who wiped her tears off his feet with her hair and "continued kissing his feet and anointing them with the ointment" (Luke 7:36–50).

The Risen Christ continues to touch us with his healing hand through our touches of each other with our healing hand. This is especially true in the marital relationship. Our gentle loving touches help break down the distance that separates us. Our human touch heals emotional hurts, fosters reconciliation and deepens our union. The human touch assuages our fears, wipes away our tears and celebrates our joys. When we touch, power goes out from us: the power of our life, the power of love, indeed, the power of Christ dwelling within us.

Touching, however, does not happen automatically. It takes time, energy, caring and sensitivity. Touching usually comes easier for those raised in a family where affection was regularly displayed in a physical way. It is more difficult for those who come from a family where this did not take place. Yet touching is so essential for creating marital intimacy. Unfortunately too many spouses have had to complain the way one wife did not too long ago, "the only time my husband touches me is when he wants sex."

COMPASSION

Luke has Jesus summing up what it means for us to be Godlike with this challenge: "Be compassionate just as your Father is compassionate" (6:36, NJB). As a Jew, Jesus was familiar with the emphasis the Scriptures of the Old Testament put on the compassion of God.

This God is the One who appeared to Moses and proclaimed: "I have observed the misery of my people who are in Egypt; I have heard their cry on account of their taskmasters. Indeed, I know their sufferings, and I have come down to deliver them from the Egyptians, and to bring them up out of that land to a good and broad land, a land flowing with milk and honey..." (Exodus 3:7–8).

This God had compassion for the Jewish people exiled in Babylon:

> For the LORD has comforted his people,
>   and will have compassion on his suffering ones.

But Zion has said, "The LORD has forsaken me,
　my Lord has forgotten me."
Can a woman forget her nursing child,
　or show no compassion for the child of her womb?
Even these may forget,
　yet I will not forget you. (Isaiah 49:13–15)

Jesus manifested this compassion of God in all of his dealings with those whom he encountered. When he toured the towns and villages and saw the crowds "he had compassion for them, because they were harassed and helpless, like sheep without a shepherd" (Matthew 9:35–36).

He multiplied the loaves and the fishes because "I have compassion for the crowd, because they have been with me now for three days and have nothing to eat. If I send them away hungry to their homes, they will faint on the way—and some of them have come from a great distance" (Mark 8:2–3).

One day as he came to the town of Nain, he saw a dead man, the only son of a widowed mother, being carried out. When he saw her "he had compassion for her and said to her, 'Do not weep.'" He then brought the man back to life and "gave him to his mother" (Luke 7:11–15).

When Mary, the sister of Martha, spoke to Jesus about the death of her brother, Lazarus, Jesus was "greatly disturbed" at the sight of her tears. He was deeply moved, and wept (John 11:32–35).

Identifying with the suffering of humans, Jesus suffered his own passion and death. "In the days of his flesh, Jesus offered up prayers and supplications, with loud cries and tears, to the one who was able to save him from death, and he was heard because of his reverent submission. Although he was a Son, he learned obedience through what he suffered" (Hebrews 5:7–8).

He is the "great high priest who has passed through the heavens." He is not "unable to sympathize with our weaknesses, but we have one who in every respect has been tested as we are, yet without sin" (Hebrews 4:14–15).

The compassion of Jesus comes alive in our lives and in our marriage through the visible manifestation of our compassion for one another. Compassion, Webster tells us, is the "sympathetic consciousness of others' distress together with a desire to alleviate it."[3] It is the ability to enter into the struggle, the pain, the anxiety, and the sorrow of others. It is the sensitivity that enables one to perceive and resonate with the hurt in another.

Lack of compassion obstructs growth in intimacy. It shuts the door to a person's attempt to communicate what is going on inside.

"Whenever I cry," one woman told me, "my husband just leaves and walks into the other room. He is totally incapable of handling it." Another man complained about his wife, "Any time I get depressed she just tells me to 'get a grip' and reminds me that I have nothing to be sad about."

To be compassionate is to listen not just with one's ears, but with one's whole being. It involves not just listening to the words another speaks, but to perceive the other's innermost feelings.

This is the greatest gift we can give to someone who is suffering. This is what heals and touches them: not a lot of words, but attentive body language that communicates nonjudgmental understanding.

"Listening," quoted in Gerald Foley's *Courage to Love...When Your Marriage Hurts*,[4] says it well:

When I ask you to listen and you start giving advice,
You have not done what I asked.
When I ask you to listen to me and you begin to tell me why I
    shouldn't feel that way,
You are trampling on my feelings.

When I ask you to listen to me and you feel you have to do something to solve my problem,
You have failed me, strange as that may seem.
Listen! All I asked of you was that you listen, not to talk or do—just
hear me.

It is this kind of compassionate response that sacramentalizes the
compassion of Jesus and deepens the bond of a marital relationship.

The greatest gift in Christian faith is that Jesus Christ, the Word
of God in human flesh, brings God down to earth. Christ is the
human face of God. To encounter Jesus is to encounter God. He is
indeed the new Temple of Divine Presence (see John 2:19–22, and
Matthew 26:61). To paraphrase Edward Schillebeeckx, Christ is the
sacrament of our encounter with God.

Marriage is a sacrament, a sign of Christ's life-giving love. To the
degree that a couple grows in their self-giving to each other in intimate love, genuine respect and unselfish generosity they become
sacraments to each other and the wider community of Christ's grace-
filled presence. As they communicate their word of faith and truth to
each other they allow the Word who is Christ to reveal himself
through their words. As they touch each other with gentle, consoling
hands they become instruments of Christ's healing touch. When they
enter sympathetically into the inner world of the other's doubts, fears
and sorrows, they allow the other to experience the compassion that
Christ has for us even in our darkest moments.

Concluding Prayer
Dear Lord, Jesus Christ,
thank you for transforming the water of our lives and our
marriage
into the new wine of your covenant.
Help us ever to be open to your grace-filled presence,
so that you may draw us closer to yourself and to each other.

May we ever listen to your Word,
so that we might be enlightened and inspired
to discover new ways of extending to one another
your healing touch and your consoling compassion.
We pray this, O loving Christ, in your name, Amen.

FOR DISCUSSION

1. One of the themes in this chapter is the author's contention that there is nothing automatic about experiencing Christ's grace in the sacrament of marriage. Christ can only transform us in our marriage to the degree to which we treat and relate to each other in a Christ-like manner. Why do you think this is true?

2. Which of the four ways describing how Christ can transform our marriage through his grace-filled presence, his Word, his healing touch, his empathy and compassion have you experienced most in your marriage and how?

3. Of these same four ways choose the one you would like to experience more in your marriage, and come up with some practical suggestions of how you think this might be achieved.

chapter two

TRINITARIAN PRESENCE

The sermon I have come to look forward to least during the liturgical year is the kind too often heard on Trinity Sunday. Last year's was somewhat typical: "The Trinity is such a great mystery it's hard to say anything about it. All we can do is believe with blind faith." Any further explanation has frequently involved little more than a repeat of the articles of the Nicene Creed. A more imaginative priest might bring in the hackneyed comparison with the shamrock, which, with all due respect to the Irish, I do not see as a very helpful analogy.

Yes, of course the Trinity is a mystery, but not in the sense of a puzzle to be solved. Rather, the Trinity is mystery because it is a divine reality that is knowable only in faith, a reality that transcends human comprehension. It is a mystery before which we can contemplatively stand in worshiping wonder.

How can we begin to talk about the Trinity? A good starting point is Jesus' testimony at the Last Supper in John's Gospel, where he outlines his experience of the Father and the Spirit.

JESUS, THE WAY TO TRINITARIAN FAITH

A major breakthrough in the history of religion was the shift from polytheism to monotheism. Rooted in the faith of Abraham, the Old Testament proclaims that the God of Israel is the one and only Supreme Being, Creator of all that is and source of all life.

This perception of God is radically transformed by the Christ event. It is through Jesus, God's Son, God's Word, that God is revealed to us as his Abba, Father. It is through Jesus Christ that we come to know the Holy Spirit who dwelt in Jesus during his earthly life and permeates his risen glory.

Jesus and the Father

In John's Last Supper discourse, Jesus proclaims an identity of union between himself and the Father. "I am in the Father and the Father is in me" (14:11). This identity is reiterated in Jesus' claim that, "All that the Father has is mine" (16:15).

Jesus also makes clear how the Father is totally involved in his ministry. "The words that I say to you I do not speak on my own; but the Father who dwells in me does his works" (14:10). "[A]nd the word that you hear is not mine, but is from the Father who sent me" (14:24).

When Jesus speaks of his death, his focus is on his return to the Father. "I came from the Father and have come into the world; again, I am leaving the world and am going to the Father" (16:28).

Who is this God whom Jesus calls Abba, Father? The Gospels have Jesus providing a number of insights:

- The heavenly Father is the one who provides for all life. God feeds the birds in the sky even though they do not sow or reap or gather into barns—how much more does God care for us! The Father clothes the flowers in the fields with greater splendor than Solomon in all his robes—how much more does God look after us! This is the one in whom we can put our trust, for the Father knows all of our needs (Matthew 6:25–34).

- The Father knows us in every detail and will never forget us. "Are not five sparrows sold for two pennies? Yet not one of them is forgotten in God's sight. But even the hairs of your head are all counted. Do not be afraid; you are of more value than many sparrows" (Luke 12:6–7).

- The God whom Jesus calls Abba is the all-forgiving One, the Good Shepherd, who, when one of the sheep is lost, leaves the ninety-nine in the desert and goes looking for the missing one until it is found. "I tell you, there will be more joy in heaven over one sinner who repents than over ninety-nine righteous persons who have no need of repentance" (Luke 15:4–7).

- Jesus' Abba is the woman who, having lost one of her ten drachmas, lights a lamp, sweeps out the house and thoroughly searches until she finds it. Her rejoicing is like the joy that takes place over one penitent sinner in heaven (Luke 15:8–10).

- The Father of Jesus is the father of the wayward son. When the father caught sight of him, he was filled with compassion, embraced and kissed him and celebrated with a feast (Luke 15:11–32).

- And this Father awaits all of us in that heavenly kingdom with "many dwelling places;" a kingdom prepared for us "from the foundation of the world" (John 14:2; Matthew 25:34).

Jesus and the Spirit

Luke has the Holy Spirit present at the very beginning of Jesus' human existence. In response to Mary's question regarding how she will conceive a son, the angel proclaimed, "The Holy Spirit will come upon you, and the power of the Most High will overshadow you; therefore the child to be born will be holy; he will be called the Son of God" (1:35).

As Jesus began his public ministry he was baptized by John at the Jordan. When he came up from the water, "suddenly the heavens were opened to him and he saw the Spirit of God descending like a dove and alighting on him" (Matthew 3:16). Then Jesus was led by the Spirit out into the desert where he fasted for forty days and forty nights (4:1–2).

After his sojourn in the desert, "Then Jesus, filled with the power of the Spirit, returned to Galilee, and a report about him spread through all the surrounding country. He began to teach in their synagogues and was praised by everyone" (Luke 4:14–15). When he went to Nazareth, he applied to himself the words of Isaiah:

> The Spirit of the Lord is upon me,
>> because he has anointed me
>>> to bring the good news to the poor.
> He has sent me to proclaim release to the captives,
>> and recovery of sight to the blind,
>>> to let the oppressed go free,
> to proclaim the year of the Lord's favor. (Luke 4:18–19)

It is this Spirit that Jesus promised at his farewell address:

> And I will ask the Father, and he will give you another Advocate to be with you forever. This is the Spirit of truth, whom the world cannot receive, because it neither sees him nor knows him. You know him, because he abides with you, and he will be in you. (John 14:16–17)

This Spirit will help them remember what Jesus had taught them.

> I have said these things to you, while I am still with you. But the Advocate, the Holy Spirit, whom the Father will send in my name, will teach you everything, and remind you of all that I have said to you. (John 14:25–26)

The Spirit will also bring to further completion the truth that Jesus had begun to communicate during his public ministry.

I still have many things to say to you, but you cannot bear them now. When the Spirit of truth comes, he will guide you into all the truth; for he will not speak on his own, but will speak whatever he hears, and he will declare to you the things that are to come. He will glorify me, because he will take what is mine and declare it to you. (John 16:12–14)

This promise to send the Spirit was fulfilled by Christ Easter Sunday evening when Jesus came and stood in their midst and breathed on them the Holy Spirit (John 20:19–23).

On Pentecost the disciples had a further experience of the Holy Spirit. There came from heaven a sound as of a violent wind. There appeared to them tongues as of fire. These came to rest on the head of each of them, and they were all filled with the Holy Spirit (Acts 2:1–4).

It is through Jesus Christ's personal relationship with God as his Father and his personal experience of the Holy Spirit within him that we have come to know God as Trinity in perfect unity.

THE TRINITY AND MARITAL SPIRITUALITY

Belief in Trinity is not just meant to involve intellectual assent. It ought to affect the way we live.[1] Of what value is right faith if it does not lead to right living (see Matthew 7:21, Luke 6:46)?

Humans, female and male, are created in the image of God (Genesis 1:27). God—Father, Son and Spirit—are united in one Divine Being. This divine unity is humanly mirrored in a unique way in the wedding of the wife and husband in mind, heart, soul and body; a wedding that merely begins at the ceremony that goes by that name, but only intensifies and deepens to the degree that the couple want to enter ever more fully into each other in intimate love and self-giving.

What follows are some suggestions of how we can allow our faith experience of the Trinity to enrich our marital journey.

Praying in a Trinitarian Way
Whether we pray alone or together as a couple, we can be aware that the Trinity is present in us and with us. God, the Father communicates God's self to us through Christ, and together they breathe into us the Holy Spirit. We can quietly contemplate this experience happening now. In praise and gratitude we open ourselves to this loving God, source of our life, and to God's enfleshed and glorified Word, Jesus Christ, and receive into ourselves this Holy Spirit. We allow the Spirit to empower us to put on the mind and heart of Christ and in, with and through Christ to become ever more united with the God whom he calls "Abba, Father."

We can most sacramentally open ourselves to the Trinity's self-giving when we participate in the Eucharist. It is here under the visible signs of bread and wine that the Father gives to us his crucified and risen Son who invites us to eat his body given for us, and drink his blood poured out for us. When we do so, we receive Christ into our innermost being where he pours the living waters of God's Holy Spirit into us.

This contemplative awareness of the presence of the life-giving Trinity in our formal periods of prayer can carry over to a deepening sense of the presence of the Trinity in the daily living out of our marital journey. In that way our entire marriage can become ever more a living prayer.

Respecting the Presence of the Trinity in One Another
The belief that God as Father, Son and Spirit dwells within us empowers us to view our marriage and our partner in new ways. These include the following.

We can see each other as an unrepeatably unique gift of God our Father, our creator, our life-giver. We accept each other as who we are as created by God, and encourage and support each other in becoming all we are called to be. This perspective eliminates any temptation we might feel to pressure our spouses into becoming something other than what they are meant to be. It calls for appreciation and affirmation of the gifts, talents and virtues that comprise the unique individuality of everyone. It involves allowing this creator God to continue the work of creating, bringing each of us closer to God's own image and likeness. As Segundo Galilea states, "The mandate of love is to let others be what they are in their deepest identity."[2]

We regard and treat one another as daughters and sons of God. This means accepting our equality as children of God, and acknowledging God, and not ourselves, as the ultimate authority. As daughters and sons of God, we are on equal ground in terms of our human personhood and our human rights. Both spouses deserve the same respect and consideration. Both are on the same footing and have equal say in regard to the marriage. Neither gender can claim to special privileges that the other does not have.

We are called to sacramentalize God's creative power in our marriage. We do this first by creating an ever more intimate, loving union in our marital relationship and an increasing atmosphere of lifegiving warmth in our home. Through our positive attitudes and actions we allow God to create in our spouse greater self-acceptance and self-confidence, deeper faith in times of doubt, greater hope when the clouds hover above. We are channels of God's creative power if and when children are meant to be a part of our marriage. We are instruments of God's creative power when we allow the strength and blessings of our own relationship to reach out beyond the borders of our home to bring new life to the lonely, the sick and dying and those deprived of the necessities of life.

We are sisters and brothers in Christ. He has taken us to himself. We are one body in him (1 Corinthians 12:12–31). We are united with him and united with one another in him. Whatever differences we may have (in temperament or ethnic, socioeconomic, educational or religious background) are small when compared to all we have in common.

We are sinners redeemed by Christ. In any mature relationship we need to be able to recognize the sinfulness, flaws, mistakes in ourselves and our partners (though, admittedly, we are usually better at recognizing the faults of others than our own). We are all redeemed by the death and resurrection of Jesus Christ. He has triumphed over sin; has been victorious over death. The sins for which we have repented are washed away. The virtues we possess we have achieved through the saving power that has been mediated through Christ. In the grace of Christ there is hope for the flaws and mistakes through which we continue to struggle.

It is vital in marriage that we see our sinfulness, faults, virtues and struggles in the light of the ongoing healing presence of Jesus Christ. Alone and together with our spouses we need to drink often from the overflowing fountains of his redeeming grace.

We are called to sacramentalize in a special way in the intimacy of our marriage the love of Jesus Christ for all of us. His love is the love of the new covenant, a love that knows no bounds, a love filled with faithful kindness, a love sealed by his death and resurrection for us. Our faith experience of Jesus' love must reflect itself in a deepening intimacy and self-giving love for each other. In turn, our growth in marital intimacy can empower us to be more fully aware of Christ's love for us and to experience his love in, and not despite, our marital relationship.

Through our baptism we share in the continuing mission of the risen Christ.[3] Through our marriage, our parenting and our reaching out to our neighbors, our parish family and the wider human community we proclaim in word and action Christ's gospel of love, and promote his kingdom here on earth.

We are temples of the Holy Spirit. The sanctifying Spirit dwells within us, empowering us to die to the sinfulness within us and to participate more fully in the life of the Trinity, a life of personal relationship and love. This makes us temples, dwelling places of the Holy Spirit. Do we really see other human beings this way? Do we truly believe that the human being is a more sacred dwelling place of the Divine Spirit than the temples we have built, the churches constructed with stones, bricks and mortar? Do we genuinely appreciate our spouses and our marriages as especially sacred dwelling places where the Holy Spirit is ever-present guiding us and transforming our relationships? Does this faith-filled perspective lead us to treat one another with greater reverence, respect and care?

The Spirit speaks to us through one another. The Spirit of God speaks to us in countless ways: through our innermost self, through the faith of our forebears and through the present community of believers. The Spirit speaks to us in a very significant way in and through the intimacy we share with our spouses. As we strive to discover God's will for us, we are called to listen to what the Spirit is saying through our spouses and in the unique context of our relationship. Of course, we must always discern the Spirit from many other spirits that can be in operation: the spirit of jealousy, of vindictiveness, of mental blindness, of selfishness, to mention only a few. But we can be helped to discern the Spirit by keeping in mind what Paul has written: "the fruit of the Spirit is love, joy, peace, patience, kindness, generosity, faithfulness, gentleness and self-control" (Galatians 5:22).

We are called to be channels to one another of the life-giving and sanctifying gifts of the Holy Spirit. Some insight into what this means can be gained by reflecting on three biblical images used to describe the Spirit. At Jesus' baptism, the Spirit of God descended upon him like a dove (Luke 3:22). A dove is a symbol of peace. Do we allow the Spirit of Peace to transform our relationships by our peacefulness and our efforts to resolve conflicts?

When speaking to Nicodemus, Jesus compared the Spirit to the wind. "The wind blows where it chooses, and you hear the sound of it, but you do not know where it comes from or where it goes. So it is with everyone who is born of the Spirit" (John 3:8). Are we open to wherever the Spirit is leading us and our relationship?

On Pentecost the Spirit appeared as tongues as of fire which separated and came to rest on the head of each of those gathered. Do we allow the fire of the Holy Spirit to burn out of ourselves and our marriage any self-centeredness, apathy and intimidation that blocks our growth in intimacy? Do we permit the fire of the Spirit ever to enkindle in us the fire of divine and human love?

Christ, who changed the water into wine, has transformed our relationship with God. Through our baptism into Christ we receive his Spirit, and by the power of the Spirit we share in his filial relationship with God. God is no longer for us merely the Supreme Being, the Almighty One, the Creator of the universe. In Christ, by the power of the Spirit, we can experience and proclaim God as our Father.

> For all who are led by the Spirit of God are children of God. For you did not receive a spirit of slavery to fall back into fear, but you have received a spirit of adoption. When we cry, "Abba! Father! It is that very Spirit bearing witness with our spirit that we are children of God, and if children, then heirs, heirs of God and joint heirs with Christ—if, in fact, we suffer with him so that we may also be glorified with him. (Romans 8:14–17)

Our faith awareness and receptivity of the presence of God as Father, Son and Spirit radically transforms our experience of each other in the marital journey and empowers us to come ever closer to the ideal for which Jesus prayed:

> ...that they may all be one. As you, Father, are in me and I am in you, may they also be in us, so that the world may believe that you have sent me. (John 17:21)

Concluding Prayer

O loving God, our Father, our Mother, our Creator,
we give you praise and thanks for creating us
and for bringing into being our marital love and unity.
Help us always to see one another as your daughter, your son.
Empower us to treat each other with the love you have for us.
Enable us to realize that what we do to each other we do to you,
and that it is to you we are ultimately accountable
for how we relate to one another in thought, word and action.

O Lord Jesus Christ
thank you for being our Savior, our Redeemer!
Be ever with us in our marriage,
empowering us to die to the dark side in each of us,
so that we might attain that depth of unity and intimacy
to which you call us.

O Holy Spirit of God,
dwell ever more deeply within us,
so that we may truly be your living temple.
Enable us to recognize and listen to you in each other,
and to become channels of your sanctifying power.

O Blessed and Loving Trinity,
Father, Son and Holy Spirit,
all praise and glory be yours
forever and ever. Amen.

FOR DISCUSSION

1. How does the belief that we are daughters and sons of God, our
   Father, and sisters and brothers of Christ affect the way we regard
   and treat each other in our marriage?

2. How does our acceptance that we are sinners redeemed by Christ
   influence our understanding and forgiveness of each other's flaws,

and our appreciation and encouragement of each other's virtues?

3. In what ways have we experienced the Spirit of Truth and Love speaking to us through the wisdom and love of our spouse?

chapter three

The Word Enfleshed

$\mathcal{T}$he most fundamental belief of the Christian religion is that the Word of God, God's very own Son, has taken on human flesh. This is what basically differentiates Christianity from the other world religions. When God wished to communicate the fullness of who God is for us, God did not remain at a distance. Instead, God's Word became one with us in human embodiment and entered fully into our humanity.

Quoting what was probably an early Christian hymn, Paul speaks of Jesus as the One

> who, though he was in the form of God,
>> did not regard equality with God
>> as something to be exploited,
> but emptied himself,
>> taking the form of a slave,
>> being born in human likeness.
> And being found in human form,

33

> he humbled himself
> and became obedient to the point of death—
> even death on a cross.

> Therefore God also highly exalted him
> and gave him the name
> that is above every name,
> so that at the name of Jesus
> every knee should bend,
> in heaven and on earth and under the earth,
> and every tongue should confess
> that Jesus Christ is Lord,
> to the glory of God the Father. (Philippians 2:6–11)

What does it mean for us that the Word of God has taken on human flesh and has become like us in all things except sin? What are some of the practical implications the incarnation has for our acceptance of our own humanity, especially in relation to our marital journey?

JESUS AND THE HUMAN CONDITION

In the year 451 the Council of Chalcedon proclaimed Jesus' humanity: "We declare that he is perfect both in his divinity and in his humanity, truly God and truly man composed of body and rational soul; that he is consubstantial with the Father in his divinity, consubstantial with us in his humanity, like us in every respect except for sin."[1]

Each of us is born with a particular ancestry and a unique genetic package. The cultural and geographic setting into which we are born also influences the course of our lives. To appreciate the humanity of Jesus we briefly recall here his lineage and the world in which he lived.

Jesus' Ancestry[2]

Matthew's genealogy of Jesus (1:1–16) doesn't read like a play in which the hero's fate is spelled out for him. It contains foreigners

(non-Israelites!) and flawed people who were involved in scandalous behavior (recorded elsewhere in the Bible). Yet, each contributed to continuing the lineage of the Messiah and thus played a role in God's plan. Tamar, who was probably a Canaanite, deceived Judah, her father-in-law, into having intercourse with her by pretending she was a prostitute. Judah later proved his hypocrisy by calling for Tamar to be burned alive when her pregnancy was discovered, until she proved that he himself had fathered her twins (Genesis 38). Rahab had been a prostitute, but she sheltered Israelite spies, making their conquest of Canaan possible (Joshua 2). Ruth, a Moabite, married Boaz after an untraditional, perhaps scandalous, courtship (see the book of Ruth). David and the Hittite Uriah's wife, Bathsheba, had an adulterous relationship. David added to his sin by arranging to have Uriah killed in battle (2 Samuel 11). Yet it was through Bathsheba's intervention that Solomon, their son, succeeded David.

Like all of us, Jesus had a mixed family tree. But even the flawed characters and irregular or scandalous unions were used by God to fulfill the messianic plan.

Human Limitations

Many Christians have more trouble accepting the full humanity of Jesus than his divinity. But if we really believe that the Word of God has become flesh, we must accept that in his humanity Jesus shared with us human limitations. Jesus' very conception in Mary's womb made him dependent on her for the nine months of gestation. He grew through babyhood, childhood, adolescence and adulthood, with all the struggles these transitions involve. Luke puts it succinctly: he grew "in wisdom and in years, and in divine and human favor" (Luke 2:52).

In his mortal humanity, Jesus was limited in time and space. He could only be in one place at a time. He had a limited amount of energy. He got tired. He had to eat and sleep. He couldn't do everything he wanted in a single day—a frustration we all share.

His human knowledge had its bounds.[3] He was, as my old history of philosophy professor used to say, a child of his time. His thinking was influenced by the worldview of his culture. He encountered the same kind of uncertainties about the future that we do.

If it is difficult to accept that Jesus' human knowledge was limited, consider how challenging it can be to think of Jesus as a sexual being (which, of course, as a human he had to be). Few sermons care to broach this subject. Yet, as Richard McBrien points out, "Jesus was fully a human being, with sexual desires and with an understanding of sexual struggle. But he subordinated (not "suppressed") the *genital* expression of that sexuality in order to leave himself completely free for the proclamation of the Kingdom of God."[4] As with all of us, Jesus' sexuality is a basic and integral dimension of who he is as a human. Acknowledging this can help us put into perspective our own struggles with the challenge of becoming fully integrated sexual human beings.

Also, like every human, Jesus knew that at some point he would have to die. He likely experienced the death of his foster father, Joseph. We know he was aware of the imprisonment and murder of his spiritual precursor, John the Baptist. The Scriptures give some indication of the depth to which he was affected by the death of his dear friend Lazarus, and his predictions about his own impending death.

The World of Jesus' Time[5]

The incarnation takes place in a very particular historical and cultural context. Biblical scholar Donald Senior brings out the importance of appreciating the environment into which Jesus was born.

> Jesus was not a mythical God whose fabled life was played out in a timeless kingdom. He was a man whose birth and life and death were bound by the observable limits of time and place. Much of what Jesus thought and said and did was shaped by and in reaction

to the culture and situation of his times. If we hope to read his portrait with intelligence and understanding, then we must know something about the thoroughly human dimensions of Jesus' world. This, after all, is part of our belief in the incarnation.[6]

Jesus was born into a land occupied by a foreign power. A Roman prefect sat in judgment in the Jewish capital city, Jerusalem. Furthermore, Jesus was a Galilean. In today's jargon that would mean he was from the wrong side of the tracks.

The northern region of Galilee was ruled by a Jewish vassal king and its population was heterogeneous. From 734 BC on it had passed through Assyrian, Babylonian, Persian, Macedonian, Egyptian and Syrian rule, infiltration and migration. In Jesus' time Galilee's population included Phoenicians, Syrians, Arabs, Greeks, Orientals and Jews. "In this mixed, commerce-oriented society, some Jews had allowed their Jewish exclusivism to weaken, but others became more militantly exclusivist. Some of the *goyim* (non-Jews) converted to Judaism and intermarried with Jews. Some religious ideas of other groups were also assimilated...."[7]

As hybrids, Galileans were looked down upon by both Gentiles and Jerusalemites.

> The Jews were scorned by the Gentiles, and the Galilean Jews were regarded with patronizing contempt by the "pure-minded" Jews of Jerusalem. The natural *mestizaje* of Galilee was a sign of impurity and a cause of rejection. The Pharisees looked down upon "the people of the land" because they were ignorant of the law. The Sadducees looked down upon them because they were somewhat lax in matters of religious attendance and familiarity with the rules of temple worship.[8]

As the Gospels testify, Galileans spoke with a distinctive accent, and the Galilean town Nazareth was a place from which no good was expected to come (Matthew 26:73, John 1:46).

Archaeological discoveries indicate that the likely population of Nazareth at the time was between three and four hundred people, and that the principal activity of the villagers was agriculture. The population of Nazareth consisted "of peasants who worked their own land, tenant farmers who worked land belonging to others, and craftspersons who served their needs."[9]

Technically Galilee was a peasant society, "meaning not only that most people worked the land but also that their productivity was extracted for the benefit of rulers without an equivalent economic recompense."[10] Taxes and rents flowed from the rural producers to the cities (especially Rome), private estates and temples.[11]

Carpenters belonged to the artisan class which constituted about five percent of Galilee's population. Artisans had a lower median income than the peasants. Because they lacked land, they could not rely on a steady food supply. The peasant and artisan classes "did overlap, however. In the villages farmers could engage in artisan work especially during the brief winter; artisan families may also have worked a plot of land."[12]

This brief overview of Jesus' ancestry, his human limitations, and the world in which he lived is meant to bring out how deeply the incarnation brought Jesus into identity with basic elements of the human condition that confront each one of us.

> Since, then, we have a great high priest who has passed through the heavens, Jesus, the Son of God, let us hold fast to our confession. For we do not have a high priest who is unable to sympathize with our weaknesses, but we have one who in every respect has been tested as we are, yet without sin. (Hebrews 4:14–15)

This faith insight gives us comfort and hope that the risen Christ is with us on our earthly pilgrimage, understanding our struggles, our mistakes and our good will in striving to do better. We now turn to how Jesus' incarnation can affect our marital journey.

THE MARITAL JOURNEY: INCARNATIONAL IMPLICATIONS

The practical implications that the incarnation has for a marital spirituality are many. We select several for consideration here.

God comes to us in and through the body of Christ. The human body is not an obstacle to divine presence, but the very vehicle through which God reveals God's intimate presence to us. In light of the incarnation, spiritualities that strive to find God by denying or trying to escape our bodiliness are misplaced. We do not have to go out of our bodies to find God. God has found us through God's Word who has become one with us. As Christians, we respond to God by receiving the body of Christ into our bodies, and in this way become radically transformed from within.[13] This personal transformation ultimately comes to fulfillment *not* in the salvation of our souls, but in the resurrection of our bodies.

Marriage is a bodily sacrament. Two inspirited body persons come together in love, and through their bodily union unite in mind, heart and soul. We call this a sacrament precisely because we believe that it is through, and not despite, our bodily sexual union that God encounters us and graces us.[14]

How well do we accept our sexuality and view it as a gift of God? Do we see sexual intimacy as something belonging primarily (or solely) to "the flesh" and having little or nothing to do with the spirit, or do we appreciate it as a significant way in which God can bring us closer not only to each other but to God's own self?

A number of the students in my college marriage course have a lot of difficulty seeing sexual intimacy as spiritually enriching and as a possible encounter with God. This is understandable on two counts. First, from their earliest years they are exposed to media depictions of sex totally divorced from permanent commitment, authentic love and regard for the effect each person has on the other. Second, many have been exposed from childhood to the negative, suspicious attitudes about sex that have been communicated through the teachings of certain churches.[15] Accordingly, getting across to the young (and not so young) the truly sacramental dimension of marital sexual intimacy, along with its concomitant responsibilities, may prove to be a difficult challenge.

In marriage we not only have to accept the strengths and flaws of our own mixed ancestry, but also that of our spouse. We all have heroines and heroes in our family tree, as well as skeletons in our ancestral closet. We need to share these with our spouse. We also have to admit the faults and mistakes of those in our heritage whom we admire the most, and the virtues and contributions made by those who were deeply flawed.

A student said to me years ago, "I really ought not be around on this planet, but I'm glad I am." When I queried what she meant, she responded, "I am the youngest of five. After four children, my mother was determined to have no more. But one night my father, a chronic alcoholic, came home drunk, forced himself on my mother, and I was conceived. So in one way I hate my father, but in another I appreciate that I am here."

A young man once revealed that he was adopted. He has never met his real mother, but learned that she had been a teenage prostitute. When she found herself pregnant, she refused to have an abortion and instead gave him up for adoption. "I love my mother and pray for her everyday, and thank God and her for giving me birth."

To be human is to have, like Jesus, a heritage both blessed and scarred. We forgive the faults, and thank God for the gifts that have come through both elements.

To accept our humanity is also to accept our human limitations and to live within them. There are four in particular that confront us all. First, we all possess certain gifts, only a few of which we have the time, energy and opportunity to develop. Humbly we acknowledge these gifts as coming ultimately from God and develop them as best we can. We also keep in mind that the talents and abilities we have are tiny, indeed, in comparison to the countless gifts we can never attain. This allows us in our marriage to appreciate and affirm the gifts of our spouse, especially those that we ourselves lack.

Second, regardless of how educated or bright in some matters we might be, our knowledge is almost nothing in comparison to what is knowable. Hence we are totally ignorant in most areas, and fallible in all spheres of knowing. Awareness of our limited knowledge enables us in our marriage to admit mistakes, to accept corrections, to avoid any indication of intellectual snobbery, and to respect and be open to the insights of our spouse.

Third, despite how hard we might try to grow in virtue and avoid hurting each other, we will never arrive at perfection this side of the grave. This ought to lead us to acknowledge our faults and express our sorrow to each other and to be determined to do better. Cognizance of our own lack of virtue should lead to greater understanding and patience with the faults of our partners.

Fourth, as the journey of marriage proceeds, we must accept the decrease in energy and the increase of fatigue and of the aches and pains that come with aging. Such changes demand appropriate adjustments to our lifestyles and to the way we relate to each other. They also increasingly bring us face to face with our mortality.

We are conditioned by the historical, cultural and religious context of the world in which we find ourselves. Obviously, dozens of books could not exhaust this topic. We here confine ourselves to only a few aspects of our contemporary situation that particularly challenge our marriage and our parenting.

We live in a world of brutal violence. There are countless wars, terrorist attacks on innocent people and the constant threat of a nuclear outbreak. Every day the news media reports the latest rapes, abductions and murders. We fear for our spouses, our children and our grandchildren. Many of the young are afraid of having children and bringing them into this seemingly terrible world.[16] This culture of violence and death casts a shadow even over the happiest of lives.

There is little cultural support for a committed permanent marriage. About half of marriages end in divorce. Many that don't are marred by incompatibility, infidelity and abuse. An increasing number of the young (and the divorced middle-aged) are choosing to live together. We are continually bombarded by the trivialization of sex in the media, the theater and the Internet.

We live in "the land of the free and home of the brave" and yet we are a nation deeply divided on what role government should play in domestic policies. In the meantime rich families get richer and poor ones get poorer even though many of them are working two jobs. The number of families without health insurance and without adequate nourishment is on the rise, and an ever-growing percentage of single mothers and their children are being driven into homelessness.

Finally, we are a nation that constitutes about six percent of the world's population and consumes about forty percent of the world's resources. The fortunate among us eat our bread under the shadow of the millions and millions around the world who are starving to death. We enjoy our abundance plagued by the awareness that much of the world lives under subhuman conditions. We are blessed with access to good health care, while fatal diseases and early death are the plight of millions on other continents.

So, an integral part of our marital spirituality is how do we respond to a culture marked by so much violence, sexual promiscuity and inhumane poverty? Our conscience constantly confronts us with the questions: Do we do enough? Do we give enough? Do we even care?

Concluding Prayer
Lord Jesus Christ, Word of God Enfleshed,
thank you for becoming one with us,
and identifying forever with our human condition.
Help us ever to find you in the bodiliness of our lives.
Empower us to become more fully human.
Enable us to realize that the more authentically human we are,
the closer we come to the Divine.
We pray this, Lord, in your name. Amen.

FOR DISCUSSION

1. Which element in the human condition of Jesus do you find most difficult to accept: his flawed ancestry, the limitations of his human knowledge or the fact that he is fully a sexual being? Why?

2. Which of your own personal human flaws and limitations do you find hardest to accept, and why?

3. What are some of the flaws and limitations in your marriage that cannot be changed? Which ones can be? How?

.chapter four.

THE PRIMACY OF LOVE

*U*nderstanding God as love is a central view of Christianity. As the First Letter of John explains:

> Beloved, let us love one another, because love is from God; every-one who loves is born of God and knows God. Whoever does not love does not know God, for God is love. God's love was revealed among us in this way: God sent his only Son into the world so that we might live through him. In this is love, not that we loved God but that he loved us and sent his Son to be the atoning sacrifice for our sins. Beloved, since God loved us so much, we also ought to love one another. No one has ever seen God; if we love one another, God lives in us, and his love is perfected in us.... Those who say, "I love God," and hate their brothers or sisters, are liars; for those who do not love a brother or sister whom they have seen, cannot love God whom they have not seen. (1 John 4:7–12, 20)

Unfortunately, this view clashes with the way God is understood by some believers. Some see God as a lawgiver who keeps track of all our failures. For others God is the one who sends natural disasters or illnesses as a punishment for sin. Some view God as the just judge ready to condemn us to the fires of everlasting hell if we die in mortal sin. For others God is the warrior on our side in our effort to destroy the enemy.

For many it is easier to believe in God than it is to believe that God is love. Maybe earlier religious training and preaching emphasized fear of an awesome God rather than trust in a loving God. For others it may be due to the lack of love in their own lives or because of tragedies that they blame on God.

Another difficulty with saying God is love is the fact we are describing one transcendent reality in terms of another transcendent reality. God is beyond any comprehension, any definition and any words. And love is a reality that defies any strict definition. Indeed, love has countless diverse meanings for different people.

Yet we all know something about love. We have experienced it in various ways. So, by analogy we can apply our experience of human love to God, and in turn, deepen our own understanding of the love we are called to have for one another in imitation of God. One essential aspect of love we focus on here is creative self-giving.

The Judeo-Christian tradition has maintained that all life comes from the loving hands of God. This belief is proclaimed throughout the Scriptures. Psalm 104 puts it in a particularly poetic way. It addresses God as the one who stretches out "the heavens like a tent" and "set the earth on its foundations" (vv. 2 and 5). The psalm continues:

> You make springs gush forth in the valleys;
>> they flow between the hills,
> giving drink to every wild animal;
>> the wild asses quench their thirst.

By the streams the birds of the air have their habitation;
   they sing among the branches.
From your lofty abode you water the mountains;
   the earth is satisfied with the fruit of your work.

You cause the grass to grow for the cattle,
   and plants for people to use,
to bring forth food from the earth,
   and wine to gladden the human heart,
oil to make the face shine,
   and bread to strengthen the human heart.
The trees of the LORD are watered abundantly,
   the cedars of Lebanon that he planted.
In them the birds build their nests;
   the stork has its home in the fir trees.
The high mountains are for the wild goats;
   the rocks are a refuge for the coneys.
You have made the moon to mark the seasons;
   the sun knows its time for setting. (vv. 10–19)

This contemplation on the glories of God's creation leads the psalmist to exclaim: "O LORD, how manifold are your works! / In wisdom you have made them all; / the earth is full of your creatures" (v. 24).[1]

God's purpose in creating is to give God's very self to us in personal love and commitment. This self-gift is manifested most fully in Jesus Christ who loved us unto death and resurrection.

This creative life-giving love of God, who is spoken of in Scripture as spouse and parent, is the model for marital love. The marriage bond is built on countless kinds of giving: the giving of oneself, of one's presence, and of one's caring. It grows in terms of the giving and sharing of things, and the giving of our energy and time to do what helps in easing the burden of the other, and in making life more manageable and more enjoyable. This kind of self-giving love not only reflects God's love, it is the instrument, the sacrament through which God gives of God's self to us, creating in us and in our relationship new life, new energy and increasing degrees of happiness.

The central place that giving has in the meaning of love is brought out in this poetic piece by John Oxenham:

> Love ever gives—
> Forgives—outlives—
> And ever stands
> With open hands.
> And while it lives—
> It gives
> For this is love's prerogative—
> To give—and give—and give.[2]

But there is a serious caution. God's love and giving is unilateral. The kind of giving love required to create marital intimacy must be mutual. Marriage is not a one-way street. It takes two to make it, one to break it.

I cringe every time I read about the scenario in which a spouse (and it has usually been the wife) complains that she does all the giving while the other does little or nothing to contribute to the marriage, and the advice given is to "double your efforts, and things will work out." Though well-intentioned, such advice is unlikely to solve the underlying problem. As Miss Tracy, my beloved second-grade teacher at St. Ignatius Loyola School in New York taught us in arithmetic class: two times zero always equals *zero*! And two times a quarter only equals a half.

A further caution: Giving is not enough. Nor is saying, "I love you" enough. We must give with love. As others have said, it is possible to give without loving, but it is impossible to love without giving. Thomas à Kempis offers this view: "The measure of love is love without measure."

GOD LOVED US FIRST

God's love is not in response to our love. Our love is in response to God's love. It is God who created us out of love for us, and who created us for love. Any power we have to love comes totally and ultimately from God. God's love for us and our love for God are mediated through our love for one another, especially through the two deepest kinds of human love that create the most profound human bonds, spousal love and parental love.

Marital and parental love are grace-filled gifts from God, that reflect God's love for us. The belief that God, out of love for us, is the creator of everything ought to make this transparent. However, our age-old suspicions in regard to sexuality, which both spousal and parental love obviously involve, have tended to cloud this truth. Clearly, the Catholic tradition is better known for acknowledging the special charism of celibacy than for giving the same recognition to marriage.

As married couples we need to ask ourselves: Do we really believe that our sexual love for one another comes from God and not from our debased and corrupted nature, as some would have us believe? If we are made in the image of God, what exists in God in a transcendent way that is reflected by our sexuality and the sexual dimensions of our love? Do we perceive God, as the Scriptures do— as spouse, mother and father? Does the experience of our own spousal and parental love help deepen our perception of the infinitely more intimate love that God has for us?

IF WE LOVE GOD AND OTHERS, GOD REMAINS IN US

The First Letter of John spells out this stark contrast, and leaves no room in between: If we love others, God remains in us; if we don't love others, we can't love God. If God is love, then loving others and being open to their love is manifesting love for God and being open to God's love. Hating others shuts God out.

The more spouses love each other, the more present God is in marriage. The quality of our love is the ultimate test of the quality of God's presence in our lives.

Pre–Vatican II thinking often gave the impression that there was a conflict between love of other humans and love of God. This was especially seen to be true of romantic love. It was as if love of God and love of neighbor were in competition with each other, and the more you loved another human the less love you had left over for God.[3] As Karl Rahner makes clear, however, love of God and love of neighbor are two inseparable aspects of the same reality.

> And yet a mutual relationship does maintain between love of God and love of neighbor, in their real mutual conditioning. There is no love for God that is not, in itself, already a love for neighbor; and love for God only comes to its own identity through its fulfillment in a love for neighbor. Only one who loves his or her neighbor can know who God actually is. And only one who ultimately loves God (whether he or she is reflexively aware of this or not is another matter) can manage unconditionally to abandon himself or herself to another person, and not make that person the means of his or her own self-assertion.[4]

The more we love God, the more deeply we love other humans. The more we grow in love of others, the more profound our growth in love of God. This applies to marital love, as well as it applies to all forms of human love.

Saint Paul reminds us of some of the characteristics of love. It expresses itself in our patience and kindness toward each other. Love "is never rude and never seeks its own advantage." It does not "rejoice at wrongdoing." Love finds joy in the truth, and "is always ready to make allowances, to trust, to hope and to endure whatever comes" (1 Corinthians 13:4–7, NJB). This kind of love totally rules out every form of name-calling, put-downs, insensitivities and every form of psychological, sexual or physical abuse. "Love requires that we refrain from everything that would harm another, and choose to do whatever will serve the other person's true well being."[5]

But, again, it must be reiterated that for a marriage to grow, such love must be mutual.

Concluding Prayer
O loving God, our Father, our Mother, our Creator,
thank you for being in an infinite way
the very essence of Love!
Thank you for being the source and foundation
of all human love!
We are grateful, Lord,
that you have made us to your image,
enabling us to be people of love.
We thank you especially
For the love in our marriage.
Empower us, we pray,
to be faithful to your image
in every aspect of our marital love,
so that we may ever grow
in union with you,
and in union with each other.
We pray this through Jesus Christ
Who lives and reigns with you forever, Amen.

FOR DISCUSSION

1. Do you have any difficulties believing that God is love? If so, what are they and what is the basis for them?

2. Do you have any problem perceiving marital sexual love as being in the image of God's love? Why or why not?

3. The author states that love of God and love of other humans are not two separate realities, but two indispensable sides of the same reality. How do you experience this in your life?

.chapter five.

AUTHORITY INVERTED

JESUS, THE SERVANT-KING

Jesus turned the customary notion and use of authority upside down. He did this by his coming and ministering as a servant even when this would culminate in his death on a cross. He also made clear that his disciples were to act accordingly.

> You know that the rulers of the Gentiles lord it over them, and their great ones are tyrants over them. It will not be so among you; but whoever wishes to be great among you must be your servant, and whoever wishes to be first among you must be your slave; just as the Son of Man came not to be served but to serve, and to give his life a ransom for many. (Matthew 20:25–28)

This model of service ran through Jesus' entire public ministry. At his baptism a voice was heard that echoed the first song of the servant in Isaiah (42:1). "This is my Son, the Beloved; my favour rests on him" (Matthew 3:17, NJB). A footnote to this verse in the *New Jerusalem Bible* states: "The immediate purpose of this sentence is to declare that Jesus is in truth the servant foretold by Isaiah, but the substitution of 'Son' for 'servant' (made possible by the double sense of the Greek word *pais*) underlines the relationship of Jesus with the Father which is that of anointed Son."[1]

This song in Isaiah that the New Testament sees fulfilled in Jesus goes on to describe the servant's role:

> I am the LORD, I have called you in righteousness
>> I have taken you by the hand and kept you;
> I have given you as a covenant to the people,
>> a light to the nations,
>> to open the eyes that are blind,
> to bring out the prisoners from the dungeon,
>> from the prison those who sit in darkness. (Isaiah 42:6–7)

When Jesus returned to Nazareth he read from another text from Isaiah that he saw being fulfilled in his ministry:

> The Spirit of the Lord is upon me,
>> because he has anointed me to bring good news to the poor.
> He has sent me to proclaim release to the captives
>> and recovery of sight to the blind,
>> to let the oppressed go free,
> to proclaim the year of the Lord's favor.
> (Luke 4:18–19; see also v. 21)

A very symbolic expression of Jesus' servant role is recorded in John's Gospel. It took place at the Last Supper when Jesus washed the feet of his disciples. According to the culture of the time, the "washing of another's feet, begrimed by travel upon dusty roads in sandals, was a menial task not required even of Jewish slaves."[2]

> [Jesus] got up from the table, took off his outer robe, and tied a towel around himself. Then he poured water into a basin and began to wash the disciples' feet and to wipe them with the towel that was tied around him.

...After he had washed their feet, had put on his robe, and had returned to the table, he said to them, "Do you know what I have done to you? You call me Teacher and Lord—and you are right, for that is what I am. So if I, your Lord and Teacher, have washed your feet, you also ought to wash one another's feet. For I have set you an example, that you also should do as I have done to you. Very truly, I tell you, servants are not greater than their master, nor are messengers greater than the one who sent them. If you know these things, you are blessed if you do them." (John 13:4–5, 12–17)

An obvious meaning of this action is the lesson that Jesus' disciples must follow his example of humble service toward one another. However, besides providing a model for discipleship, this symbolic action takes on further meaning in light of Jesus' death the next day. It was clear on that Thursday night that the enemies of Jesus were determined to have him put to death because of the way he ministered. They were disturbed by his preaching, his calling God his "Abba," his healing on the Sabbath, his claim to forgive sin and his association with the "unclean." In doing a task reserved for a slave Jesus reiterated his acceptance of the servant role that would culminate in suffering and death.

As Raymond Brown points out, the footwashing is "a prophetic action symbolic of Jesus' passion and death.... In demeaning himself to wash his disciples' feet Jesus is acting out beforehand his humiliation in death.... The footwashing is an action of service for others, symbolic of the service he will render in laying down his life for others..."[3]

In describing the passion and death of Jesus the four gospels make allusions to the third and fourth servant songs of Isaiah and see Jesus as the fulfillment of the Suffering Servant.[4] The familiarity that most have with the passion narratives bring to mind the similarities between the description of Jesus' suffering and some of the verses in these songs.

I gave my back to those who struck me,
and my cheeks to those who pulled out the beard;
I did not hide my face from insult and spitting. (Isaiah 50:6)

He was oppressed, and he was afflicted,
yet he did not open his mouth;
like a lamb that is led to the slaughter,
and like a sheep that before its shearers is silent,
so he did not open his mouth.

...

They made his grave with the wicked
and his tomb with the rich,
although he had done no violence,
and there was no deceit in his mouth.

....

Out of his anguish he shall see light;
he shall find satisfaction through his knowledge.
The righteous one, my servant, shall make many righteous
and he shall bear their iniquities. (Isaiah 53:7, 9, 11)

The paradox is that in becoming the Suffering Servant, Jesus exercises true authority, inverting completely the worldly concept of power. This is brought out in the crucifixion scene where over the tortured, dying body of Jesus is nailed the proclamation, "Jesus of Nazareth, King of the Jews." In contrast to the power, wealth and fame that goes with worldly kingship, Jesus on the cross is totally helpless, stripped of everything, even his garments, and is executed in disgrace. Yet it is precisely by becoming the Suffering Servant and completely giving of himself in sacrificial love that Jesus is glorified. By exercising his kingship in this manner Christ influences the minds and hearts of his followers down through the ages and into eternity.

SERVICE, AUTHORITY AND MARRIAGE

There are three basic structures of the exercise of authority in marriages: patriarchal, matriarchal, partnership. The patriarchal, where the husband rules and the wife obeys, is a model that predominates down through the ages, although admittedly, a few cultures have been matriarchal.

Partnership marriages are on the rise in some cultures today, especially in North America and Western Europe. (I was speaking of these three types in a lecture sometime back, and a woman raised her hand and said: "there is a fourth type, like my marriage, where I rule but let him think he does!")

In our marriage the preference is for the model described by the bishops at the Second Vatican Council: marriage as an intimate partnership of life and love.[5] However, whichever pattern a couple adopts, Jesus' exercise of authority through loving, sacrificial service ought to be the example that inspires the way the couple relate to one another. Such a following of Christ will manifest itself in a number of ways.

Both enter and live the marriage in order to serve, not to be served. Their love moves them to want to do whatever they can to make life easier and happier for the other. The countless tasks involved in running a household and rearing children are assigned not on the basis of gender stereotype (which in reality always favors the male), but on the basis of mutual agreement and sharing the burdens.

One woman complained a while back, "When I got married, I went from being a maiden to becoming a maid." Another shared the story of her teenage son. When she asked him to clean the toilet he refused saying, "That's woman's work." Taking him firmly by the collar, with toilet brush in hand, she responded, "No, that's not woman's work, it's human work. Humans use the toilet; they can also clean it."

Whenever I think of Jesus washing his disciples' feet, there immediately comes to mind the countless ways in which that symbolic, ancient action translates in a contemporary marriage: washing dishes, cleaning clothes, changing dirty diapers, scrubbing floors, dusting furniture and vacuuming carpets, to name just a few.

Reflecting on that Last Supper scene can make these chores less dreary and inspire more cheerful, loving action. If both spouses approach their service this way, so many arguments would cease, so much resentment would be assuaged, and the marital journey would become far more pleasant.

Giving orders and making demands are replaced by consultative discussions and polite requests. Consultation and discussion imply respect and sensitivity for the feelings and wishes of the other. The goal is not to do "my will" but to discover "our will," not to get "my way" but to follow "our way."

One word transforms a demand to a request—"please." From their earliest years, whenever any of our three daughters wanted anything, my wife and I always first asked, "What's the magic word?" Habits are formed very young! But it's never too late to try to teach this lesson, or to take it to heart ourselves.

A story from the late Indian Jesuit, Anthony de Mello, is apropos: "The Master offered the perfect solution to a married couple who was forever quarreling. He said, 'just stop claiming as a right what you can ask for as a favor.' The quarreling instantly stopped."[6]

One can have much more influence on the other when complaints and negative criticisms are situated in a positive context. Any negative comment ought to be in the context of many affirmative ones. A counselor I know tells her clients that for every complaint there ought to be ten compliments; for every flaw you need to point out, you should affirm ten good things about the person. I don't know how strictly mathematical we want to get on this, but the basic point is well made. Sometimes in our family, we have sat around the table after dinner, and each person took a turn saying all the things they liked about each family member. Sometimes on a birthday we have done that for the birthday celebrant. It's tremendously affirming of the individual and bonding for the family.

The second aspect is one that is mentioned in almost any book

on communication, but worth repeating here. When we point out
something that annoys us it is much more effective to use "I" statements rather than "you" statements. "I feel put upon when you leave
your dirty dishes in the sink for me to do," goes much further than,
"You lazy slob, you leave a mess wherever you go." With "I" statements, we take responsibility for our own feelings. "You" statements
come across as accusatory and put others on the defensive.

Finally, any correcting of our spouses ought to be done with a
humble awareness of our own faults and eccentricities. This leads to
greater understanding, patience and tolerance.

Concluding Prayer
Lord, Jesus Christ,
we give you thanks, praise and glory
for being our Servant King.
Teach us, we pray,
to exercise our influence on our spouse
and on our children
not by "lording it over them"
but by mutual respect,
sensitive concern
and loving service.
We pray this, Lord,
in your name. Amen.

FOR DISCUSSION

1. The author states that Jesus became king by becoming the suffering servant. What meaning does this statement have for you?
2. Is the dominant authority structure in your marriage patriarchal,
matriarchal or partnership? What do you find satisfactory and/or
unsatisfactory in that model?
3. How do you personally experience the author's basic premise that
the most effective exercise of authority in a marriage is through
loving service?

chapter six

SUFFERING AND DEATH TRANSFORMED

*E*ven in the best of marriages the blessings are mixed with disappointments, the joys are laced with sufferings, new life is accompanied with a variety of dyings. Our belief is that Jesus Christ, who shared to the fullest our sufferings and death, has given radically new meaning to both, not only for himself but also for all of us. We examine here the tribulations and triumphs of marriage in light of Jesus' victory over pain and death.

THE JESUS EXPERIENCE

We tend to limit the sufferings of Jesus to Holy Thursday night and Good Friday. The Gospel narratives, however, record a series of sorrows, rejections and disappointments throughout his public ministry for which Calvary was but the culmination.

Early in his ministry Jesus returned to Nazareth, went to the synagogue, read an Isaian text and then spoke to those gathered. After they heard his message "all in the synagogue were filled with rage. They got up, drove him out of the town, and led him to the brow of the hill on which their town was built, so that they might hurl him off the cliff. But he passed through the midst of them and went on his way" (Luke 4:28–29).

Jesus lost his beloved cousin John the Baptist to a cruel and violent death. Herod had John arrested, chained, imprisoned and beheaded. When Jesus received this news he withdrew with some of his disciples to a place where they could be by themselves (Matthew 14:3–13).

Jesus was the object of many serious charges. One of the most damning was the accusation that he was possessed by Beelzebul, the prince of devils (Mark 3:22). On two occasions the negative reaction to Jesus' teaching was so strong that his hearers took up stones to throw at him (John 8:59, 10:31).

It was not just with his enemies that Jesus had problems. He knew misunderstanding and rejection from those who had been close to him. Some of his own relatives tried to have him put away. After his "Bread of Life" discourse in John's Gospel "many of his disciples turned back and no longer went about with him" (John 6:66). He was betrayed with a kiss by Judas, who then committed suicide. He was denied three times by Peter.

As his ministry progressed, Jesus had to face the prospect of his own death. But his was no ordinary dying. He was arrested, falsely charged and condemned to execution. He was mocked, scourged and crowned with thorns. He was crucified as a criminal, and rejected by the highest authorities of his own cherished religion.

By accepting rejection, suffering and death with forgiveness and love he conquered the sinful hatred that had condemned him.

He committed no sin,
    and no deceit was found in his mouth.
    When he was abused, he did not return abuse; when he suffered,
    he did not threaten; but he entrusted himself to the one who
    judges justly. He himself bore our sins in his body on the cross, so

that, free from sins, we might live for righteousness; by his wounds you have been healed. For you were going astray like sheep, but now you have returned to the shepherd and guardian of your souls. (1 Peter 2:22–25)

By rising from the dead he has forever transformed the meaning of death.

But in fact Christ has been raised from the dead, the first fruits of those who have died. For since death came through a human being, the resurrection of the dead has also come through a human being; for as all die in Adam, so all will be made alive in Christ. But each in his own order: Christ the first fruits, then at his coming those who belong to Christ. (1 Corinthians 15:20–23)

Out of the depths of his profound suffering and death, Jesus has been raised to new life, and has promised the same for us. We now explore the implications that Jesus' death and resurrection have for the marital journey.

MARRIAGE: THE CHALLENGE AND THE HOPE

Christian spirituality is centered on the crucified and risen Christ. Both aspects need to be kept together. It is significant that after the resurrection when Jesus appeared to his disciples, they saw him in his risen glory *with his wounds* (John 20:24–28). This is a wonderful image for Christian couples to keep in the forefront of their contemplative minds. It is precisely through his acceptance of suffering, rather than abandoning his mission and compromising his personal integrity, that Jesus is glorified. His wounds can never be eclipsed, but they are forever gloriously transformed.

In his own glorified state Christ transforms his followers. In his post-Resurrection appearances he shared his Spirit and brought radical change to his disciples. From misunderstanding him during his public ministry, they came to new perceptions. From abandoning him on that Thursday night, they followed him even to their own death. Peter, the triple denier became the triple proclaimer of his love for Christ (John 21:15–17). Thomas the disbeliever was confirmed in his faith. Paul, who did not know Jesus during his public ministry, was forever changed through his encounter with the Risen Christ. From being a persecutor of Christians he became an apostle to the Gentiles. Finally, through their death in fidelity to Christ they share forever in his risen glory.

So it is with us. The crucified and Risen Christ is with us transforming our marital journey. There are the normal range of hardships, hurts and pain that go with any marriage. We must make a living, do multiple tasks and manage the countless minutiae that are embedded in everyday married life. Despite our best efforts there are occasional unavoidable misunderstandings. Our intimate love does not insulate us from unintentional hurts. We experience disappointments, loss of jobs, various injuries and illnesses, old age and ultimately death itself.

There are changes in each of us and in our relationship as we move down the lifelong road of our marriage. We grow from post-honeymooners through the first several critical years, which for most include the advent of children. We move through the middle years and maybe "a midlife crisis," whatever form that might take. At some point we gradually go from a full household to an empty nest. For not a few that nest may not remain empty for too long, depending on what difficulties may confront our adult daughters and sons. Parenting never ends. We then move on together through the middle years into senior citizenship, perhaps retirement and then into old age.

This is the picture, if we are lucky. But there are millions who have not been so fortunate. Instead of these transitions bringing the couple closer together, many have been driven apart. The high divorce rate attests to this sad reality. The lives of so many others are marked with unexpected challenges and heartbreaking tragedies:

chronic unemployment, children with birth defects, death of a child, marital infidelities, abuse and the early death of a beloved spouse. Many of these wounds will never completely heal.

But whatever our journey, be it one marked with the normal range of problems, or one marred by tragedy, Christian faith provides us with the awareness that the crucified and Risen Christ is with us, at the door knocking. Do we allow him in?

Neither the normal wear and tear of the journey nor the scars of the tragic wounds can be prevented. But they can be transformed. It is all in how we respond.

Hanging in my office is an attractive card with a quote attributed to Paul Claudel. It reads: "Jesus did not come to explain away suffering or remove it. He came to fill it with his presence." When confronted with sorrows, small or large, we are tempted to ask, "Why did God will this?" Or, "Why did God allow it?" These may be the wrong questions, for all the speculation in the world can never provide a satisfactory answer this side of the grave. The better question is: What is the will of God for me now in light of this particular set of circumstances, regardless of how the situation came about? How, in other words, can I respond to these realities in my life in ways that keep intact my personal integrity rather than compromise it? How can we as a couple grow in faith and love with God and each other as we respond to the ordinary and extraordinary trials and tribulations?

Two thoughts are relevant here.

1. *It is helpful to situate the tough and sad times, the disappointments and even the tragedies in the context of our past personal experience of God's love and care for us.* Too often we tend to isolate the bad times from the good and wind up seeing God in negative ways. The author of Psalm 22 provides a more positive approach. He is a person seriously ill and oppressed by his enemies. His prayer begins, "My God, my God why have you forsaken me?" The psalmist then addresses his own question. He places his present trials in the context of the history of his ancestors.

Yet you are holy,
>   enthroned on the praises of Israel.
In you our ancestors trusted;
>   they trusted, and you delivered them.
To you they cried, and were saved;
>   in you they trusted, and were not put to shame. (vv. 3–5)

The psalmist then reflects on his own personal history.

Yet it was you who took me from the womb;
>   you kept me safe on my mother's breast.
On you I was cast from my birth,
>   and since my mother bore me you have been my God.
Do not be far from me,
>   for trouble is near
>   and there is no one to help. (vv. 9–11)

As subsequent verses make clear, these remembrances do not magically take away his problems. They do, however, help him turn to God with faith and trust. The concluding theme of the psalm is one of praise and a sense of fulfilled hope.

I will tell of your name to my brothers and sisters;
>   in the midst of the congregation I will praise you:
You who fear the LORD, praise him!
>   All you offspring of Jacob, glorify him;
>   stand in awe of him, all you offspring of Israel!
For he did not despise or abhor
>   the affliction of the afflicted;
he did not hide his face from me,
>   but heard when I cried to him. (vv. 22–24)

It is significant that the New Testament records Jesus praying the beginning of this psalm as he died on the cross (Matthew 27:46). As a devout Jew, Jesus undoubtedly knew well this entire psalm.

A prayer shared with me some years ago reflects this same insight of seeing the difficult times in light of the good.

> Lord, as this day unfolds, help us to see the creations of beauty you have bestowed upon us. It can be easy for us to let ourselves be overwhelmed with sorrow because of the hard times we may face, and consequently much of the good that surrounds us is overlooked. Please Lord, help us to keep our minds open to see the good things in life so that we may focus on the rainbow, not the storm; that we may see the rose, not the thorns. And when night falls, may it be not the blackness that overwhelms us, but the beauty of the majestic stars. For, when we focus on the goodness and love that exists, we can fully appreciate the wonderful gift of life you have blessed us with, and when we concentrate on the love that is present, we radiate love and celebrate your love for us.[1]

Recalling the blessings in our life not only helps us cope with present sorrows, it makes us less fearful of the future. Our experience of God being with us during the past dark periods of our life gives us hope that God will never abandon us and will be with us, whatever lonely roads and dark nights might mark our future journey. A saying attributed to Ralph Waldo Emerson comes to mind: "For all I have seen, I trust the Creator for all I have not seen."

2. *As a Christian couple our prayer in time of sorrow can be deeply comforting by keeping in mind the image of the crucified and Risen Christ.* He is God's Son, but this did not make him immune from profound suffering. It is not that God directly willed the suffering. What God willed was that Jesus proclaim the kingdom of God, even though it was inevitable that humans would reject him and put him to death. But God was there with him on the cross giving him the strength to endure human-inflicted sufferings with his personal integrity intact. And God raised him up from the seeming final destruction of Good Friday into the glory of risen life on Easter Sunday.

It is thus with us as we travel our earthly pilgrimage. God does not "send" us difficulties and trials. They are built into the marital journey. But our Christian faith enables us to be aware that God and Christ are with us in our darkest hours, giving us the strength to work through our sufferings, empowering us to preserve our personal integrity, and raising us from the ashes of our dyings into new life now and for eternity.

Concluding Prayer
We turn to you, Lord Jesus Christ,
our crucified and risen Savior.
We give you praise and thanks
for passing through death into new life.
You give us hope for the journey,
whatever may lie ahead.

Be with us, we pray,
that through all the dyings
we may grow in new life,
until that day when we are forever
united with you in your risen glory.
We pray, this, Lord, in your name. Amen.

FOR DISCUSSION

1. What was one of the most difficult and trying events in your married life thus far?
2. How did you experience the presence of God and of Christ leading you to new life through that dark hour?
3. What possible sad event in your future journey do you dread the most? How does your past experience of new life through suffering give you hope to endure what comes?

chapter seven

Earthly Marriage and the Eternal Wedding Feast

One of the images that Jesus used for the kingdom of heaven was a wedding feast (see Matthew 22). In this parable the required garb is a wedding garment. The book of Revelation reflects a similar theme of marital imagery in its description of heaven.

And from the throne came a voice saying,
> "Praise our God,
> all you his servants,
> and all who fear him,
> small and great."

Then I heard what seemed to be the voice of a great multitude, like the sound of many waters and like the sound of mighty thunderpeals, crying out,
> "Hallelujah!
> For the Lord our God
> the Almighty reigns.

> Let us rejoice and exult
> and give him the glory,
> for the marriage of the Lamb has come,
> and his bride has made herself ready;
> to her it has been granted to be clothed
> with fine linen, bright and pure"—
> for the fine linen is the righteous deeds of the saints. (19:5–8)

In this chapter, we reflect on two aspects of the intimate communion in the heavenly kingdom that are foreshadowed in a loving marriage. These can tell us not only something about heaven, but also can underscore the importance they have for a happy sacramental marriage. The two aspects I choose here, unity and peace, are based on the prayer to Christ recited before the Sign of Peace at the Eucharist.

> Lord Jesus Christ, you said to your apostles:
> I leave you peace, my peace I give you.
> Look not on our sins, but on the faith of your Church,
> and grant us *the peace and unity of your kingdom*
> *where you live for ever and ever.*[1]

The peace and unity of Christ's kingdom are built on sinlessness, harmonious acceptance of diversity and intimate communion.

SINLESSNESS

After greeting each other with a peace gesture, the congregation prays, "Lamb of God, you take away the sins of the world, have mercy on us, grant us peace." This taking away of sin is more than merely forgiveness in the sense of not holding our sins against us. It is ultimately a radical cleansing of our being from all sinfulness, all alienation from God and others. It is the kind of cleansing that Isaiah has God proclaim: "[T]hough your sins are like scarlet, / they shall be like snow; / though they are red like crimson, / they shall become like wool" (1:18). This cleansing involves an inner transformation, as God's word through Ezekiel makes clear: "I will sprinkle clean water upon you, and you shall be clean from all your uncleannesses, and from all your idols I will cleanse you. A new heart I will give you, and a new spirit I will put within you; and I will remove from your body the heart of stone and give you a heart of flesh" (36:25–26).

In the life of heaven all sin has been forever taken away. Not only has everyone there been totally forgiven, they have been purified of all their faults. They are totally converted, fully turned toward God and one another in the perfection of love. They dwell in complete unity and peace.

This gradual conversion begins now here on earth. The elbow-to-elbow living together in marriage and family gives us a special opportunity and challenge to deal with the sinfulness and faults of one another. Do we let all the flaws and hurts get on our nerves and build barriers between us, or do we tear down the walls that divide us by admitting our sinfulness, being repentant and determined to do better? Do we allow our impatience, intolerance and resentments to drive us apart, or do we work toward that inner conversion that fosters mutual forbearance, understanding and intimate communion?

Diversity

Heaven is the ultimate communion of saints. There women and men from every age, race and nation, from every creed and religious background, from the entire span of the educational and socio-economic spectrum are forever united. Seeing God "face to face" as the creator, redeemer and sanctifier of all humans will empower us in heaven to see each other as God does. The differences that divided us in our sinfulness on this earth will then be seen as diverse reflections of the inexhaustible beauty and goodness of the one God of us all. The diversities that tend to fragmentize us now will form one wonder-full mosaic redounding forever to the glory of God.

This harmony in heaven is a model which we are called to emulate here on earth. The first place for this to happen is in one's marriage and family. If it cannot be achieved here, how can it be achieved in the neighborhood, the nation, the global community?

In a marriage two different people accept each other and embark on the journey toward oneness. This involves embracing the opposite gender and confronting all the pockets of sexism that reside deep in the human psyche. It includes accepting differences in backgrounds, personality, beliefs and values, however minor or major these may be. Where there are children we are called to let go and allow each to grow according to their own pace and along the diverse paths God calls them.

This acceptance of diversity in marriage and family life frees us to be more tolerant of the differences that exist in the wider community, and to experience now a little bit of a taste of the harmony that will exist in perfection in the eternal kingdom.

INTIMATE COMMUNION

In heaven we achieve the fullest possible communion with God through Christ by the power of the Spirit. This intimacy with God is not something experienced in isolation but in communion with all of God's people. This profound intimacy with God and one another is finally achieved by letting go of the fear of losing oneself and of leaving what is known for what is unknown. This ultimate abandonment of these fears takes place in death as we commit ourselves to the hands of God in that unseen future.

The closest personal intimacy that we can experience in this life is in a happy loving marriage. This intimacy is sacramental of the intimacy with God which finds its fulfillment in the heavenly kingdom. Each day of our marriage we commit ourselves to an unknown future. We conquer our fears and recommit ourselves to this growing intimacy with one another in God and in Christ. We let ourselves go, believing that it is in "losing" ourselves that we "find" ourselves. This leaving behind the past and embracing an unknown future leads us to new vistas of understanding and love that foreshadow and prepare us for that ultimate surrender of ourselves that brings us to the newness of life and intimacy in the heavenly kingdom.

Another text in the book of Revelation uses marital imagery to describe God's kingdom.

> Then I saw a new heaven and a new earth; for the first heaven and the first earth had passed away, and the sea was no more. And I saw the holy city, the new Jerusalem, coming down out of heaven from God, prepared as a bride adorned for her husband. And I heard a loud voice from the throne saying,
> "See, the home of God is among mortals.
> He will dwell with them;
> they will be his peoples,
> and God himself will be with them;
> he will wipe every tear from their eyes.
> Death will be no more;
> mourning and crying and pain will be no more,
> for the first things have passed away." (21:1–4)

We foretaste the day of this eternal wedding feast in our marriage each time we wipe away each other's tears, and turn one another's mourning into gladness, and heal and comfort each other in our pain. Truly, then, in this way we become God's people, and God makes God's home among us, and we experience the peace and unity of Christ's kingdom where he lives now and forever.

Concluding Prayer
Thank you, God, for enabling us
to experience your presence in our marriage.
Empower us, we pray,
to allow you to dwell more deeply in our relationship.
Help us give witness to your kingdom
by living in harmony, peace and love with one another.

Lead us through our marital journey
to that place which you have prepared for us

from the beginning of time.

We ask this through Jesus Christ our Lord

who lives and reigns with you forever. Amen.

For Discussion

1. In one paragraph write out your imagined description of heaven. Which elements of this description do you already experience, though imperfectly, in your marriage?

2. What do you think are a few practical changes of behavior on the part of the both of you that could make your marriage an even greater taste of the life of heaven?

part two

Marriage as a Unique Vocation

n this section of the book I wish to reflect on Christian marriage as a God-given vocation, rooted in our baptismal call. To some
it might seem superfluous to stress these two realities. Don't we
already know that every state of life is a vocation? Are we not aware
that there is a link between the sacrament of matrimony and that of
baptism, since it is clear that no one can receive the Christian sacrament of matrimony, unless they are already baptized?

But do we truly realize that marriage is a vocation? Cerebrally we
can give a "yes" to that question. However, do most Catholics really
appreciate the significance of this reality in ways that are clearly manifest in our practice? Let's think about it. How often at the Prayer of
the Faithful at Mass when prayers for vocations to religious life,
priesthood, diaconate and lay ministries are said, have you heard the
vocation of marriage included? Some of us who attended Catholic
high schools in the forties recall vocation talks that left the clear
impression that if you had sufficient intelligence, health and moral
uprightness, you were called to priesthood and religious life. If you

were not generous enough to follow that call, you got married. This inferior view of marriage was then supported by quoting Saint Paul (1 Corinthians 7:8–9, NJB) out of context: "To the unmarried and the widows I say that it is well for them to remain unmarried as I am. But if they are not practicing self-control, they should marry. For it is better to marry than to be aflame with passion."

Furthermore, even if we acknowledge marriage as a divine vocation, do we understand fully enough the fact that it is deeply rooted in our baptismal call? This, in turn, leads to the deeper question regarding the meaning of baptism and the quality of life to which it challenges us.

I have treated elsewhere the call to marriage as grounded in our baptismal vocation.[1] For the purposes of this book I wish to focus on three dimensions of the meaning of baptism that are, unfortunately, omitted in the renewal of baptismal promises that we make at the Easter Vigil and at the conferring of the sacrament of baptism. The first dimension calls us to be open to the Holy Spirit who enables us to enter ever more fully into the death and resurrection of Jesus Christ. The second bids us to pursue the fullness of holiness. The third challenges us to participate in the mission of Christ. As we reflect on these aspects of baptismal life, we will then probe the unique ways we are called to live these out in our vocation of Christian marriage.

chapter eight

BE OPEN TO THE SPIRIT

*I*n this chapter we reflect on one of the central meanings of baptism, namely the gift of the Holy Spirit who empowers us to share in the death and resurrection of Christ by dying to our sinfulness and to live in Christ. Baptism, however, is not merely a past event. It is a lifelong process. The giving of the Holy Spirit that we sacramentally received in our baptism is not a once-and-for-all static gift, but a dynamic grace. The Spirit continues to be with us, endeavoring to transform us into the image of Christ. The baptismal call for us is to be open to the Spirit and to allow this Holy Spirit to bring about continued conversion in our mind, our heart and our soul.

Those of us who are called by God to the sacrament of Christian marriage are challenged to live this baptismal openness to the Spirit in and through the unique dimensions that constitute the journey of marital intimacy. The way of Christ for us is to be led by the Spirit in the ongoing process of dying to the sinfulness and darkness within us that stands in the way of growth in the intimate exclusive love that constitutes the marital union. It is this dying that gives way to new birth of life and love with each other in Christ.

Do you not know that all of us who have been baptized into Christ Jesus were baptized into his death? Therefore we have been buried with him by baptism into death, so that, just as Christ was raised from the dead by the glory of the Father, so we too might walk in newness of life. For if we have been united with him in a death like his, we will certainly be united with him in a resurrection like his. We know that our old self was crucified with him so that the body of sin might be destroyed, and we might no longer be enslaved to sin. For whoever has died is freed from sin. But if we have died with Christ, we believe that we will also live with him. We know that Christ, being raised from the dead, will never die again; death no longer has dominion over him. The death he died, he died to sin, once for all; but the life he lives, he lives to God. So you must also consider yourselves dead to sin and alive to God in Christ Jesus. (Romans 6:3–11)

Of the countless dyings and risings that living our baptism requires, three are chosen here because of their special relevance to married life. Dying to selfishness, patriarchal entitlement and a spirit of rivalry gives way to living more fully a life marked by generosity, equality and cooperation. In our treatment we reflect on how each of these are lived out first in the wider community and then in unique ways in our marital relationship.

FROM SELFISHNESS TO GENEROSITY

At the start, it is important to define clearly what I mean here by selfishness. Selfishness is not love of self. In fact love of neighbor implies love of self, as Jesus' mandate to love one's neighbor as oneself indicates. Nor is selfishness to be confused with thinking of oneself and protecting and caring for oneself. You have to take care of yourself if you are going to be in condition to take care of others. Finally, it is not selfish to think well of oneself. Psychologists make clear that having a good self-image is a prerequisite for thinking well of others, for engaging in mature communication, and for taking the risk of giving of oneself in love.

Selfishness, as the term is used here, means thinking primarily of oneself, with little or no concern for the needs or wishes of others. It is seeking one's own interest at the expense of others. It is pursuing what I want to do or what I wish to acquire, regardless of the harm or destructiveness this causes other people.

Our United States culture is full of countless examples of this kind of me-first selfishness. We must be the number one, most powerful nation in the world, even if it means initiating wars or boycotts that cause havoc to masses of people, especially women and children. We must have the greatest economy even if it causes the scandalous imbalance of approximately 6 percent of the world's population consuming about 40 percent of its resources. We are a country that supports political and economic polices that empower the rich to get richer ("that's fine; they have worked hard for it; they deserve it"), and cause the working poor to get poorer ("that's their fault; they are just too lazy to pull themselves up by their own bootstraps.")[1] We tolerate the sexual exploitation of women in our advertising and our pornography, as long as it brings in the money. To gain wider audiences we promote violence, vulgarity and exhibitionism in our entertainment, regardless of the effects this has on our collective consciousness and on the minds and hearts of our youth. And we listen without objecting as our presidents and politicians publicly limit their prayer to "God bless America" rather than "God bless the world."

This national attitude that we are number one, that we must be first, affects our one-to-one relationships with each other. The competitive TV reality shows encourage the thinking that anything goes in order to get ahead: lying, cheating, deceit, betrayal, crushing the other person, making it to the top on the bones of those who have been disposed of. So, in the lives of many, one must get good grades even if it means plagiarizing; one must win the game at any cost even if it involves taking steroids or trying to injure the opposing player; one must "climb the ladder of success," even if to get there, others must be thrown off.

Unless we are careful, this me-first drive that permeates our culture can affect our marriage. Hence, a number of self-reflective questions are in order. In our marriage is my ongoing disposition to consider myself first, or to be ever conscious of myself *and* my spouse? In our marital relationship do I think "I" or "we?" In all the areas of our marriage, including workloads, finances and sexuality, am I primarily concerned about my own personal self-interests, or am I equally sensitive to the desires and feelings of my spouse?

We live out our baptismal vocation in marriage by opening ourselves to the Spirit of God's covenantal love and kindness. It is this Spirit who empowers us to die to our self-centeredness, to any meanness, stinginess and lack of concern within us, so as to live in a spirit of generosity and self-giving that enables us to think of our spouse at least as much as we think of ourselves. It is such openness to the Spirit that enables us to grow in the kind of marital intimacy that sacramentalizes the covenantal love of God and of Christ.

FROM PATRIARCHAL ENTITLEMENT TO EQUALITY

Since the time of the first sin, as described in Genesis 3, the man has pointed the finger of accusation at the woman, and has sought to dominate her (see vv. 12 and 16). Indeed, one of the most pervasive sin of the human race has been the idea of male superiority and dominance. For millennia women have been treated as if they were the property and playthings of men. Even in our more enlightened age, the plight of women around the globe continues to instill horror. In 2000, the United Nations reported that:

> Girls and women worldwide, across lines of income, class and culture, are subjected to physical, sexual and psychological abuse.

Violence against women includes rape, genital mutilation and sexual assault; forced pregnancy, sterilization or abortion; forced use or non-use of contraceptives; "honour" crimes; sexual trafficking; and dowry-related violence.

Around the world, at least one in every three women has been beaten, coerced into sex, or abused in some other way—most often by someone she knows, including her husband or another male family member. One woman in four has been abused during pregnancy.[2]

This report goes on to specify that as many as five thousand women and girls are put to death annually in so called "honour killings," many of these because they had been raped. Approximately four million females are bought and sold worldwide each year, "either into marriage, prostitution or slavery."[3] At least a hundred and thirty million women have been forced to undergo female genital mutilation or cutting.[4]

In this country alone some three to four million women a year are beaten by their husbands, male lovers and exes. More than a third of all female homicide victims are killed by their husbands or boyfriends. A woman is raped every six minutes. Twenty-five percent of the abused women in the United States are battered during pregnancy, most of them attacked in the abdomen.[5]

Patriarchal entitlement also reflects itself in less dramatic ways. The sociologists tell us that in this country women make about two-thirds of the salary that men in comparable positions make, and in about seventy percent of the households where both spouses are working outside the home, the wife is still expected to do most of the household tasks and child rearing.

The first place where we can live out our baptismal commitment to be open to the Spirit and die to the sinfulness of patriarchal superiority and the domination of women is in our marriage. Because of the millennia of sinful exploitation and abuse of women, the residue of prejudice against them resides deep inside the collective consciousness, and this has affected each of us in one way or another. In a marriage both the husband and wife have to face this dark side of the human race. Where do we stand, deep within ourselves, regarding the basic equality of both genders? Do we both really believe that on the level of our existence we have the exact same human dignity and fundamental rights? Are we truly convinced that if marriage is to be an intimate partnership, then spouses must be on an equal plane in regard to all the elements that constitute the matrimonial way of life?

If so, then we are called to examine how these beliefs translate into action. Is equal respect given to the rights each of us has to become all we are called to be? Are the insights, opinions, wishes and desires of each spouse regarded with equal seriousness? Are both spouses true partners in the decision-making processes? Is there a fair distribution of labor? Is each of the couple given equal opportunity to pursue their career, to associate with their friends, and to enjoy their interests and hobbies? Our answer to these questions will indicate to what degree the practice of our marriage reflects the baptismal belief that we are both equal members of the one Body of Christ (1 Corinthians 12:12–31) and that "there is no longer male and female; for all of you are one in Christ Jesus" (Galatians 3:28).

FROM RIVALRY TO COOPERATION[6]

Hanging in my office at home is a large reproduction of Ted DeGrazia's famous painting *Los Niños*. It depicts eleven children from diverse ethnic backgrounds holding hands in a lively circular dance. I love this picture because it visualizes for me what God's dream for the human race must be, namely, that we be in a circular dance, hand-in-hand with each other, rather than "climbing the ladder of success" at the expense of others, and even throwing them off the ladder altogether. This vision of the human circular dance is in harmony with the dance of the universe, the dance of the galaxies and solar systems. It is in imitation of the God of the dance in Zephaniah 3:17: Your God "will rejoice over you with happy song, / he will renew you by his love, / he will dance with shouts of joy for you, / as on a day of festival" (NJB).

If we were all open to the Spirit of the God of the Dance there would be an end to all wars, all murders and all harmful actions that destroy the bodies, minds, hearts and souls of ourselves and others. It would strike the death knell to every kind of hatred and empower us to rise into the love of Christ that embraces all human beings. This openness to the Spirit would give us the inspiration and the grace to put aside all bitter rivalries and enter the great circular dance.

And where does this begin? Certainly in our intimate relationships. In marriage all rivalry ought to give way to our holding hands in a circular dance. Instead of pitting my gifts, my talents, my intelligence, my prowess against that of the other, we join our gifts, our minds, our hearts, our spirits together in a bond that no other force can break. Our marriage becomes a circular dance, where the better you dance, the better I dance; where the better I dance, the better you dance. And together we perfect our circular dance of sharing, self-giving and boundless love.

But it is not always that easy. It takes two to dance. The spirit of rivalry dies slowly. Shortly after I got married, a friend, pointing to his wife, gave me some advice. Raising his hand a short distance from the floor he said, "You raise them up so high, and only so high!" About the same time another male acquaintance warned me: "Tell the women very little; the more you tell them, the more they will get in your way." Luckily my wife and I had already entered the circular dance, and so were impervious to such morsels of nonsense.

The dance, however, is never perfect. It takes the lifetime journey to keep making it better. There are three areas in particular in which we can ask ourselves how well we do the circular dance. Am I jealous of the talents in which you excel and I lack? Or do I support, encourage and rejoice in your gifts, and appreciate what they contribute to our marriage?

Am I able to cope and be happy with your having a more prestigious and better-paying job than I do? Women have been used to this for millennia. With opportunities changing today, it might be harder for some men. I remember a male student several years ago saying to me that he could never marry a woman who made more money than he. Another male student who overheard him retorted, "I will take whatever money I can, whoever brings it in."

Do we compete for the affection and attention of our children? Am I put out because a child gets along better with you than with me? Do we play the children against the other spouse? Or do we really co-parent and work together in a united front for the nurturing and well-being of our children?

God is the God of the dance. The universe is in one great dance. The more successful we are in engaging in the circular dance of our marriage, the more we imitate the God of the dance, and contribute to the dance of the universe and the circular dance of the human family. Therein, indeed, lies the salvation of the world.

Concluding Prayer
Thank you, God, for the gift of your Spirit,
given sacramentally in our baptism.
Help us appreciate that our marriage
is a true vocation rooted in our baptismal call.
Empower us to be ever open to your Spirit
that we might more fully die
to selfishness, gender inequality and destructive forms of
    rivalry,
so that we may become more generous,
equal and cooperative partners to one another,

and to the wider community of our church and our human
society.

We pray this through Christ our Lord. Amen.

FOR DISCUSSION

1. What does it mean to you in your daily life to be open to the Spirit and share more fully in the death and resurrection of Christ?

2. How do you experience your marriage as a true vocation that flows from your baptismal commitment?

3. Of the three examples of our dark side discussed in this chapter (selfishness, patriarchal entitlement, destructive forms of rivalry) which is the one you struggle with the most in your marriage, and how do you try to meet that challenge?

chapter nine

PURSUE THE FULLNESS OF HOLINESS

When those of my generation were growing up, we were given the impression that there was a divide in the church between the "ordinary" Christian on the one side, and priests and religious on the other. The former were called to keep the commandments and save their souls, while the latter were called to be holy.

Fortunately, the Second Vatican Council, in chapter five of *Lumen Gentium*, "The Universal Call to Holiness," corrected that misunderstanding. "It is therefore quite clear that all Christians in whatever state or walk in life are called to the fullness of Christian life and to the perfection of charity, and this holiness is conducive to a more human way of living even in society here on earth" (40). The bishops continued:

> The forms and tasks of life are many but there is one holiness, which is cultivated by all who are led by God's Spirit and, obeying the Father's voice and adoring God the Father in spirit and in truth, follow Christ, poor and humble in carrying his cross, that they may deserve to be sharers in his glory. All, however, according to their own gifts and duties must steadfastly advance along the way of a living faith, which arouses hope and works through love. (41)

The Council then specifically addressed the married state:

> Christian married couples and parents, following their own way, should with faithful love support one another in grace all through life. They should train their children, lovingly welcomed from God, in Christian doctrine and evangelical virtues. Because in this way they present to all an example of unfailing and generous love, they build up the community of charity and stand as witnesses to and cooperators in the fruitfulness of mother church, as a sign of and a share in that love with which Christ loved his bride and gave himself for her. (41)

Talk about the fullness of holiness and the perfection of love always leaves us with an open question. What are some of the specific characteristics that constitute this state of saintly love? An adequate answer to this would be almost limitless. For our purposes here we focus on five aspects of holiness mentioned in Matthew's version of the beatitudes: being poor in spirit, gentleness, mercy, being pure in heart and peacemaking (5:3–9).

POVERTY OF SPIRIT

In contrast to Luke where the beatitude is for "the poor," Matthew has added the words "in spirit." Poverty in spirit, then, applies to the rich and middle class and not just to the economically deprived. It means that in our lives spiritual values are more important than material ones, that God's concerns for the good of humanity are of greater priority than economic gains, that the well-being of other people comes before the accumulation of wealth.

This virtue of poverty in spirit has many applications to married life. First, it has us look at our priorities and assess whether nurturing the marital and parental relationships is more important than making money. When the two are in conflict we need to face the decision of whether we sacrifice the job advancement or the opportunity to make more money in order to preserve and deepen the family relationships, or vice versa.

This virtue has us live within our means and be satisfied with a moderate style of living. It leads us to measure our worth not in terms of our material possessions, but in the quality of our personhood. It involves our realizing that the ultimate owner of all creation is God, to whom we are accountable for our stewardship of the material gifts we have been granted.

Finally, poverty in spirit inspires us to share in Christ's love for and identity with the underprivileged (Matthew 25:40). It makes us concerned about unjust employment conditions and unfair compensation for the working poor. It leads us to take a stand on behalf of the voiceless, and to share whatever we can of our goods with those less fortunate.

GENTLENESS

Saint Paul refers to the gentleness of Christ (2 Corinthians 10:1), and to gentleness as one of the fruits of the Spirit (Galatians 5:22). In Matthew's Gospel the words of Isaiah (42:2–3) are seen fulfilled in Jesus: "He will not wrangle or cry aloud, / nor will anyone hear his voice in the streets. / He will not break a bruised reed / or quench a smoldering wick " (Matthew 12:19–20).

Some of the aspects of being gentle that Webster notes are vital in a marriage. Negatively, it is being "free from harshness, sternness, or violence." On the positive side, it includes being "kind" and "amiable."[1]

The more intimate a relationship the more one is vulnerable. A special effort, therefore, has to be made in a marriage to avoid anything that can be hurtful to the other. We must avoid harsh thoughts, offensive words and mean actions. Gentleness excludes every type of rudeness and insensitivity.

Being gentle, however, goes beyond avoiding what causes hurt. The positive side of it can be surmised from our wider life experiences. "Handle with care! These items are very breakable," read the sign in old Mrs. McGrane's gift and china shop in the town where we often summered in my youth. "Be kind to the plants, they will live longer," were the instructions handed out by a florist I used to know. The entrance to the children's section of a zoo cautioned: "Be gentle when petting the animals, they are more fragile than they look."

In marriage we live this gentleness by handling each other with care, and by being sensitive to the effect our words and actions have on the other. Kindness, thoughtfulness and imagination empower us to relate in ways that give life to each other and ensure the longevity of our marital intimacy. Expressing ourselves tenderly in all the physical demonstrations of our affection and love respects and safeguards the fragility that resides in the psyche of each of us. Doing all this will number us among the gentle who, indeed, are truly blessed.

MERCY[2]

One of the very powerful parables of Jesus is that of the unforgiving debtor. A servant owed his king ten thousand talents (equivalent to over sixty million dollars). When he could not pay he was ordered to be sold with his family and possessions to pay off the debt. At the servant's plea the master felt sorry for him and cancelled the debt. Later the servant met a fellow servant who owed him a hundred denarii (less than two hundred dollars), and had him thrown in prison until the debt was paid (Matthew 18:23–35). The lesson is obvious. As we receive mercy, we should give it in return.

Our Judeo-Christian tradition has us firmly believe in the mercy of God. In Psalm 51:1 we pray, "Have mercy on me, O God, / according to your steadfast love." At the beginning of the Eucharist we turn to Christ, "Lord, have mercy. Christ, have mercy. Lord, have mercy." At countless times we pray for forgiveness of our sinfulness and deliverance from our plight. And like the psalmist we are convinced we are heard. "The Lord answered me / when I called in my distress" (Psalm 120:1, NAB).

We extend to our spouse and children the mercy we have received from God each time we avoid any kind of vengeance, and instead, make allowances for their mistakes and faults, give correction without personal condemnation, and forgive as we have been forgiven.

But mercy, as Webster points out, also includes giving relief from distress. It call us to be there with understanding, comfort and support whenever any family member is suffering anguish of mind, heart or soul.

PURITY OF HEART

As *The New Jerome Biblical Commentary* points out, this term has diversified meanings in the Scriptures. In the Old Testament it "refers to ritual and moral impurity being cleansed." In Matthew "it stands close to justice and includes covenant fidelity, loyalty to God's commands, sincere worship."[3]

We can go beyond these meanings as we apply this term to marriage. Purity of heart is linked with purity of intention, with singleness of purpose. It means that what we do in regard to our spouses we do for the right reason. And the right reason must always be an authentic love that contributes to the genuine good of the other. This rules out duplicity, manipulation and mind games. What you see is what you get. Our agenda is laid out on top of the table. No one has to look underneath to discover the real motives.

PEACEMAKING

I am always impressed that this beatitude is not for the *peacekeepers* but for the *peacemakers*. That is a very important distinction, especially for the marital relationship. True peace is built on justice, on the regard and respect of the equal rights of others. Peacekeeping works at preserving a superficial tranquility, even if injustice and violation of personal rights are festering underneath. It would have us put on a false face even when being stabbed in the back, so we do not ruffle any feathers. It would have us act in a calm way while boiling deep inside, because we are afraid of what might happen if we open our mouths. But that is not genuine peace. Hostility, anger and hatred will simmer under this façade, and will finally explode in ways we would prefer to avoid.

Peacemaking, on the other hand, involves confronting injustice even though it will make the perpetrators angry and cause a great deal of conflict, at least temporarily. Peacemakers will always pay a price for their efforts.

Jesus is a wonderful example of the cost of peacemaking. In Luke's infancy narrative the heavenly throng celebrated his birth by proclaiming peace on earth (2:14). On the other hand, Simeon asserted that he was destined "to be a sign that will be opposed" (2:34). Jesus' public ministry bore out that prediction. He confronted in no uncertain terms the religious leaders for their hypocrisy (Matthew 23:13–36). He also took on the temple establishment which had turned "a house of prayer" into "a den of robbers" (Luke 19:45–46). Because of such confrontations, opposition to Jesus became so intense that he ultimately paid the price of his life.

The more intimate the relationship, the harder it can be to confront the loved one with traits that disturb you, with actions that are unfair, with feelings that you are being taken advantage of. Over the years I have heard a number of statements that go like this: "I am afraid to confront my wife about her drinking, because if I do she will go into a tirade." "I don't dare criticize my husband about his abusive language toward me, because it will only make matters worse." "I wind up doing all the dirty work around the house, but if I complain my spouse will tell me I am just making a martyr of myself. So I just grin and bear it."

The reluctance to confront is understandable. It is very difficult and is rarely done without some upheaval. It is only, however, in standing up against evil and injustice that true peace can be made. If we do, the reward is great, for as the beatitude proclaims, it is in

being peacemakers that we will be recognized as children of God
(Matthew 5:9).

Concluding Prayer
Lord Jesus Christ,
you have called us through baptism
to the fullness of holiness, the perfection of love.
Aid us in our vocation of marriage
to be true to our baptism
and grow as a holy and loving couple.

Help us to see each other and our relationship
as far more important than the accumulation of riches.
Inspire us to treat each other
with your mercy and your gentle kindness.

Let all we do be done with purity of intention,
out of love and regard for each other.
Guide us in our conflicts to conduct ourselves
in ways that create your peace.
We pray this, O Lord, in your name. Amen.

FOR DISCUSSION

1. How do you experience your marriage as a call to the fullness of
   holiness?
2. Of the five virtues that are the focus of this chapter which one
   manifests itself most fully in your marriage, and how?
3. Which one of these five do you see as most lacking in your relationship? What are some of the practical ways in which you can
   grow in this area?

chapter ten

PARTICIPATE IN THE MISSION OF CHRIST

*T*oo often in the past, active sharing in the ongoing mission of Christ was identified with ordained ministers and religious. The Second Vatican Council disabused us of that notion. Speaking of the laity, *Lumen Gentium* states: "all the faithful, that is, who by baptism are incorporated into Christ, are constituted the people of God, who have been made sharers in their own way in the priestly, prophetic and kingly office of Christ and play their part in carrying out the mission of the whole Christian people in the church and in the world" (31).

In this chapter we will reflect on how Christian marriage is a call from God to live in a special way our baptismal commitment to carry out this threefold ongoing mission of the crucified and Risen Christ.

THE PRIESTLY MISSION

Come to him, a living stone, though rejected by mortals yet chosen and precious in God's sight, and like the living stones, let yourselves be built into a spiritual house, to be a holy priesthood, to offer spiritual sacrifices acceptable to God through Jesus Christ....

But you are a chosen race, a royal priesthood, a holy nation, God's own people, in order that you may proclaim the mighty acts of him who called you out of darkness into his marvelous light. (1 Peter 2:4–5, 9)

In their chapter on the laity in *Lumen Gentium* the bishops at the Second Vatican Council pick up on this Petrine theme.

Since he wishes to continue his witness and his service through the laity also, the supreme and eternal priest, Christ Jesus, gives them life through his Spirit and ceaselessly impels them to accomplish every good and perfect work.

To them, whom he intimately joins to his life and mission, he also gives a share in his priestly office of offering spiritual worship for the glory of the Father and the salvation of humanity. Hence the laity, dedicated as they are to Christ and anointed by the Holy Spirit, are marvelously called and prepared so that ever richer fruits of the Spirit may be produced in them. For all their works, if accomplished in the Spirit, become spiritual sacrifices acceptable to God through Jesus Christ: their prayers and apostolic undertakings, *family and married life*, daily work, relaxation of mind and body, even the hardships of life if patiently borne (see Pet 2:5). In the celebration of the Eucharist, these are offered to the Father in all piety along with the body of the Lord. And so, worshipping everywhere by their holy actions, the laity consecrate the world itself to God. (34, emphasis added)

For our purpose here we will focus on three of the aspects of a married couple's call to share in the priesthood of Christ as outlined by the bishops: spiritual worship, spiritual sacrifice, and the offering of the Eucharist.

Spiritual Worship
Worship is first of all an attitude that resides in the depths of our mind, heart and soul. In our marital union we acknowledge that God is the creator of human sexuality, gender and the reality of marriage itself. Hence, we strive to discern God's will for us in this important dimension of our life. We do not conduct ourselves according to our own whims, but make every effort to discover where God is directing us in our relationship and to have the strength to follow that lead.

As Christians we consciously open ourselves in our marriage to the presence of God through Christ by the power of the Spirit. We experience in faith and gratitude the companionship and friendship of our trinitarian God in our companionship and friendship with each other. We acknowledge the grace of God working in us through our mutual graciousness with one another. We rejoice with God's confirming presence in good times, and find comfort in God's soothing presence when we must walk through the dark valley of disappointment, sadness and heartbreak (see Psalm 23:4).

We visibly offer worship to God when as a couple, as a family we join our minds and hearts—and sometimes our hands—and pray together.[1] We place our lives in the hands of God. We give thanks for the love we experience and all the blessings that are showered upon us. We place our trust in the Divine Presence as we face an always unknown future. We pray for guidance in the many crossroads of our journey, and for protection from the myriad evils that lurk everywhere in our very troubled world.

Our acknowledgment of God as the author of our marriage, our openness to the presence of the Trinity in our relationship, and our celebration of this in prayer together are three of the significant elements that constitute our priestly ministry of worship.

Spiritual Sacrifice
In the passage from *Lumen Gentium* quoted previously, family and married life are specified as among the works that "if accomplished

in the Spirit, become spiritual sacrifices acceptable to God through Jesus Christ." This means that our whole marriage can be an offering of ourselves to God through the offering of ourselves to each other.

We solemnly initiate this offering at the wedding ceremony, and reaffirm it with every act of love toward our spouse: our kind words, our thoughtful gestures, our sensitive courtesies, our daily tasks, our struggles, our times of relaxation and enjoyment, our shared meals, and the giving of ourselves in sexual intimacy. All that is done in the Spirit of truth and love is a pleasing sacrifice to God and renders us and our relationship increasingly sacred (*sacrum facere*). We become evermore an acceptable sacrifice to God, in and through Christ, by the power of the Holy Spirit.

In this way we fulfill in the context of our marriage and family life the directive that Paul gave to his converts in Rome:

> I appeal to you therefore, brothers and sisters, by the mercies of God, to present your bodies as a living sacrifice, holy and acceptable to God, which is your spiritual worship. Do not be conformed to this world, but be transformed by the renewing of your minds, so that you may discern what is the will of God—what is good and acceptable and perfect. (Romans 12:1–2)

The Eucharist

We liturgically exercise our share in Christ's priesthood when we join the community of our fellow Christians in the celebration of the Eucharist. It is there that in a public way we unite the worship and sacrifice of our daily lives, and offer them in union with the crucified and risen Christ: this is my body given for you, this is the cup of my blood poured out for you.

This liturgical exercise of our priesthood as a baptized people is described by the bishops at Vatican II in the Constitution on the Sacred Liturgy (*Sacrosanctum Concilium*). In the early part of the document, speaking of liturgy in general, the bishops state:

Christ, indeed, always associates the church with himself in this great work in which God is perfectly glorified and men and women are sanctified. The church is his beloved bride who calls to its Lord, and through him offers worship to the eternal Father.

The liturgy, then, is rightly seen as an exercise of the priestly office of Jesus Christ. In the liturgy the sanctification of women and men is given expression in symbols perceptible by the senses and is carried out in ways appropriate to each of them. In it, complete and definitive public worship is performed by the mystical body of Jesus Christ, that is, by the Head and his members.

From this it follows that every liturgical celebration, because it is an action of Christ the priest and of his body, which is the church, is a preeminently sacred action. No other action equals its effectiveness by the same title nor to the same degree (7).

Later on in this same document, the bishops focus their attention specifically on the Eucharist. Having described how the eucharistic sacrifice is a memorial of Christ's death and resurrection (47), they go on to say:

The church, therefore, spares no effort in trying to ensure that, when present at this mystery of faith, Christian believers should not be there as strangers or silent spectators. On the contrary, having a good grasp of it through the rites and prayers, they should take part in the sacred action, actively, fully aware, and devoutly. They should be formed by God's word, and be nourished at the table of the Lord's Body. They should give thanks to God. *Offering the immaculate victim, not only through the hands of the priest but also together with him, they should learn to offer themselves.* Through Christ, the Mediator, they should be drawn day by day into ever more perfect union with God and each other, so that finally God may be all in all. (48, emphasis added)

In our eucharistic liturgy there are several rituals that celebrate what we have striven to do in our daily marriage, and that strengthen and inspire us to go forth to live it even better in the days to come.

The liturgy begins with a confession of our faults and omissions, followed by a request for and a granting of forgiveness. We bring to this ritual all the wrongs we have committed and celebrate liturgically the apologies and pardons we have already shown each other. In turn we go back to our daily routine more deeply reconciled.

In the liturgy of the Word we allow Christ to speak to us through the reading of the Scriptures. Having heard the Word of God we go forth to live it in our family life.

Through the Offertory and Consecration we offer our lives in union with Christ, so we may return to our household and be more fully the Body of Christ for one another.

At the Sign of Peace we symbolically express to each other our wish for tranquility of mind and heart, and pledge that in the week ahead we will be for each other channels of Christ's peace.

We enter sacramentally into communion with Christ by eating the eucharistic bread and drinking the eucharistic cup, so that Christ might be more deeply present to us in our lives, in our marriage and at our family meals.

Finally, we are sent forth with God's blessing, so that we might return to our homes and be more fully a blessing for those whose lives we touch.

We share, indeed, in a special way Christ's priestly mission when we celebrate the Eucharist, and then go out and live it.

THE PROPHETIC MISSION

A prophet is one who proclaims God's truth to the people of his time. Jesus came in the wake of Moses and the other great prophets of Israel. He is, however, seen in the New Testament as greater than Moses and the prophets. *Lumen Gentium* describes Jesus' prophetic mission this way:

Christ is the great prophet who proclaimed the kingdom of the Father both by the testimony of his life and by the power of his word. Until the full manifestation of his glory, he fulfils this prophetic office, not only through the hierarchy who teach in his name and by his power, but also through the laity. He accordingly both establishes them as witnesses and provides them with an appreciation of the faith (*sensus fidei*) and the grace of the word (see Acts 2:17–18; Apoc 19:10) *so that the power of the Gospel may shine out in daily family and social life.* (35, emphasis added)

The document later goes on to address specifically the prophetic vocation of married people.

The state of life that is sanctified by a special sacrament, namely, married and family life, has a special value in this prophetic office. Where the christian [sic] religion pervades the whole structure of life, constantly and increasingly transforming it, there is both the practice and an outstanding school of the lay apostolate. *In it the married partners have their own proper vocation: they must be witnesses of their faith and love of Christ to each other and to their children.* The christian [sic] family proclaims aloud both the virtues of the kingdom of God here and now and the hope of the blessed life hereafter. (35, emphasis added)

Two of the aspects of the prophetic mission that the bishops stress in the above texts are giving witness to our faith and love of Christ to each other and our children, and allowing the power of the gospel to shine out in our daily family and social life. Here we see that while a distinction can be made between the priestly and prophetic mission, there is an overlap. Certainly one of the ways in which we give witness of our faith and let the gospel shine forth is through our priestly worship and offering of sacrifice. Presupposing this, let us explore some of the other ways in which we can give witness to our faith in Christ and allow our following of his gospel to be manifest in our married and family life.

1. We confess our faith to one another. We let our spouse and our children know what we believe and why we believe it. We allow them to see who Christ is for us, and how that influences our deepest convictions and the way we live. We communicate with our spouse our questions, our doubts, our faith struggles, and through our mutual understanding and support encourage each other. We listen with tolerance to our children as they express their own faith difficulties to us. We appreciate the fact that it is only through the painful process of questioning that they can grow in their own faith development.

2. We share our moral principles and spiritual values, especially those that regard the dignity of every human person, and those that relate to human life issues, social justice and human sexuality. The operative word here is "share." It is futile and counterproductive to try to impose these values on someone else. But by the way we ourselves live the very values we proclaim we have an influence that goes beyond words.

3. Spouses can support each other's growth in their faith by providing opportunities for retreats and adult religious education programs. They can also encourage one another to read articles and books that deepen faith understanding and provide a Christian perspective on current issues. One couple told me, "Our Christmas shopping for one another is very simple. Each year we give each other the money for at least a three-day retreat. Sometimes we make it alone and sometimes together." Another couple confided that each year on their wedding anniversary they give each other a spiritual enrichment book.

4. We provide for the formal religious education of our children. While the primary place for faith formation is in the home, it is also important for parents to see that their children are exposed to good religious instruction in their parish church or school. Where these do not provide adequate religion programs, parents should exercise their rights and their power to insist that the religious education of their

children receive the same professional expertise as demanded by other ministries and other academic disciplines.

5. We must strive to live in everything we do the Gospel mandate that is summarized in the Golden Rule: "In everything do to others as you would have them do to you" (Matthew 7:12). This is so simple, and yet so difficult because it is all embracing. But how radically all our lives would be changed if this one rule were followed.

Proclaiming this central truth must begin in our marital relationship and in our parenting. Do we always act toward our spouse and our children the way we wish them to act toward us? Only if we model this, can we insist that our children do the same.

Some time ago I visited a family and observed a common happening with a not-too-common parental response. The two-year-old hit his three-year-old sister and took her toy. Milking it for all it was worth, she went weeping and screaming to her parents. The boy was not scolded on how naughty he was. Nor was he sent to his room or deprived of dessert. The father gently took him aside and let him realize how he had made his sister cry. He then asked him how he would have liked it if his sister had done the same thing to him. When the boy reluctantly and sheepishly acknowledged he would not have liked it, he was instructed to apologize to her. It was touching to see this little one go and hug his sister and say, "I'm sorry."

6. We are called to proclaim the gospel beyond the walls of our home. We can do this by teaching in parish religion programs, or participating in adult Bible or faith-sharing groups. Most of all we do it by relating to all people, regardless of race, ethnicity, or faith persuasion, in a manner consistent with the teaching and example of Jesus Christ.

THE KINGLY MISSION
The bishops of Vatican II remind us that Christ, obedient to death and exalted by the Father, has entered into the glory of his kingdom and continues to exercise his kingly mission through us.

> The Lord desires that his kingdom be spread by the lay faithful
> also: the kingdom of truth and life, the kingdom of holiness and
> grace, the kingdom of justice, love and peace. In this kingdom, cre-
> ation itself will be set free from the slavery of corruption and will
> obtain the glorious freedom of the children of God. (*Lumen
> Gentium*, 36)

In chapter seven we reflected on the connection that Jesus made
between the wedding feast and the kingdom of heaven. We probed
how we can already experience God's reign in our marriage and family life and how this can be a foretaste of the fullness of God's reign
in the life we call heaven. In other parts of this book we have shown
how many of the virtues associated with God's kingdom, like the ones
mentioned in the passage quoted above, are essential in creating a
happy and holy marriage. All the efforts we make to manifest these
qualities in our marriage indeed further the kingdom and reign of
God proclaimed by Jesus.

In this present reflection we take another approach. We look at
the kingly mission in terms of doing what Jesus says we must do here
on earth in order to enter the kingdom of heaven:

> [H]e will put the sheep at his right hand and the goats at the left.
> Then the king will say to those at his right hand, "Come, you that
> are blessed by my Father, inherit the kingdom prepared for you
> from the foundation of the world; for I was hungry and you gave
> me food, I was thirsty and you gave me something to drink, I was
> a stranger and you welcomed me, I was naked and you gave me
> clothing, I was sick and you took care of me, I was in prison and you
> visited me." Then the righteous will answer him, "Lord, when was
> it that we saw you hungry and gave you food, or thirsty and gave
> you something to drink? And when was it that we saw you a
> stranger and welcomed you, or naked and gave you clothing? And
> when was it that we saw you sick or in prison and visited you?" And
> the king will answer them, "Truly I tell you, just as you did it to one

of the least of these who are members of my family, you did it to me." (Matthew 25:33–40)

These actions that Jesus prescribes for entrance into his kingdom have special relevance to marriage and family, and this for two reasons. First, providing food, drink, clothing and healthcare are essential for satisfying some of the basic needs that all humans have, and the family is the primary place where these needs have to be cared for. Second, these actions constitute a major portion of the time and energy that go into maintaining a household. Too often cooking, washing dishes and clothes and taking care of a sick spouse or child are seen as mere routine tasks and, consequently, their spiritual dimension is missed. If we truly believe, however, that when we perform these actions "for the least of these" (and this surely includes our family members) we do them for Christ, they become a living prayer, and are deeply linked with making Christ's kingdom present here on earth.

As we care for the needs of our family in the name of Christ we are reminded that his kingdom extends far beyond the walls of our home, and that God's family includes all our sisters and brothers throughout the planet. So, we are also called to share in the work of his kingdom by being aware of and reaching out to the millions who each day are starving, who walk around in rags, who are dying in the streets without any medical provisions and with no one who cares for them. The kingdom of Christ embraces all human beings and every need they have.

Concluding Prayer
We worship you, Lord Jesus Christ.
You are our Priest, our Prophet, our King.
We thank you for calling us through our baptism and our
  marriage

to share in unique ways in your priestly, prophetic and kingly
mission.

Give us the wisdom, the courage and the generosity
to participate to the fullest in this threefold ministry of yours,
until we join you forever in your heavenly kingdom.
We pray this in your name. Amen.

FOR DISCUSSION

1. What are some of the ways in which you personally see yourselves
   and your family as a priestly people?

2. How as a couple can you share more fully in your prophetic mission of sharing your faith with each other, your family and your
   parish?

3. To what degree do you experience the ordinary tasks of providing
   and preparing food, clothing and healthcare for each other and
   your children as having a spiritual dimension and advancing
   Christ's kingdom?

chapter eleven

SOME LITURGICAL IMPLICATIONS

*T*he way we pray ought to manifest our faith understanding and, in turn, reinforce it. Unfortunately, the present liturgical forms of the baptismal promises and the wedding vows reflect none of the positive aspects of these two sacraments as inspired by Vatican II. Hence, in concluding this portion of the book I wish to analyze these present liturgical texts and suggest possible ways in which they could be enriched, so as to remind us of what these two sacraments ought to mean in our lives, as well as inspire us to go forth and live them more fully.

BAPTISMAL PROMISES

One of the rituals at the Easter Vigil and at the Eucharist on Easter Sunday is the renewal of baptismal promises. In the introduction to this ritual the priest reminds the congregation that "through the paschal mystery we have been buried with Christ in baptism, so that we may rise with him to a new life." The participants are then invited to renew "the promises we made in baptism when we rejected Satan and his works, and promised to serve God faithfully in his holy

Catholic Church."[1] The celebrant then goes on to ask three questions: "Do you reject Satan?" "And all his works?" "And all his empty promises?" To each of these the congregation responds, "I do."

If the priest wishes, he can replace those questions with an alternative set: "Do you reject sin, so as to live in the freedom of God's children?" "Do you reject the glamour of evil, and refuse to be mastered by sin?" "Do you reject Satan, father of sin and prince of darkness?"[2]

While the latter set of questions is slightly less jejune than the former, neither brings out any of the specifically distinctive Christian elements of baptismal life. Indeed, most believers of other religions could give a resounding yes to the essence of all the above questions. Accordingly, this renewal ritual misses a tremendous opportunity to recall what it truly means in positive terms to be a baptized Christian. I would like to suggest here some of the *kinds* of questions that could better achieve this goal:

- Are you willing to participate in the death and resurrection of Christ by dying more fully to your sinfulness and self-centeredness, and by growing in your personal union with him and in your love for others?
- Do you commit yourself to be open to the Holy Spirit to inspire you in the decisions you make and in the way you live your life?
- In your personal relationships with others will you be guided by the Spirit of Christ's truth, love and service rather than the spirit of deceit, apathy and selfishness?
- In your business dealings will you be motivated by the well-being of others rather than by monetary greed?
- In facing conflicts will you avoid psychological and physical abuse and follow the path of peacemaking and reconciliation?
- Are you committed to share in Christ's mission of feeding the hungry, caring for the homeless and ministering to the sick and the needy?

• Will you do what you can to spread Christ's kingdom by changing the sinful societal structures that entrap the deprived and
the oppressed, so that they may experience the freedom of the
children of God?

This list is not intended to be used blindly. The number of questions
and their wording could be adapted to what is deemed suitable in a
particular setting. What these types of questions could do is to
remind congregants of the practical implications of being baptized,
and inspire them to live their baptismal life more consciously. From
a catechetical standpoint this is particularly appropriate, since almost
the only time a large percentage of Catholics go to church are at
Easter and the baptism of relatives and friends, the very occasions
when the renewal of baptismal promises is officially called for.

MARRIAGE VOWS

The official rite of Catholic marriage offers two formulas for the marriage vows. The first reads: "I, N., take you, N., to be my wife (husband). I promise to be true to you in good times and in bad, in sickness and in health. I will love you and honor you all the days of my
life." An alternate formula can also be used: "I, N., take you, N., for
my lawful wife (husband), to have and to hold, from this day forward,
for better, for worse, for richer, for poorer, in sickness and in health,
until death do us part."[3]

The first formula contains more positive elements than the second one, but neither make any reference at all to the Christian
dimension of marriage. There follows three of the ways in which
these formulas could be improved:

1. The idea of "taking" the other as one's spouse would best be
replaced with the concept of *giving* oneself as spouse to the other,
and *receiving* the other's self-gift as spouse.

2. Mention ought to be made of entering the marriage as a vocation from God that is rooted in one's baptism. This can be done by the couple renewing their baptismal promises immediately prior to proclaiming their marriage vows, and then connecting their marriage vows with their baptismal call.

3. In light of the Catholic church's insistence that marriage between two baptized persons is a sacrament, it is totally incongruous that the present form of the marriage vows contains not the remotest allusion to that sacramentality. The formula needs to include the couple's commitment to live their marriage in a way that reflects Christ's presence in their lives, and to love each other as Christ loves us.

There is certainly more than one way in which these three suggestions can be incorporated into the wedding ceremony. What follows is intended as a mere sample of linking a renewal of baptismal promises with the pronouncing of the marriage vows:

O Loving God,
today with the help of your grace,
we renew our baptismal commitment
to be open to your Holy Spirit in our lives,
and to follow more closely your Son, Jesus Christ.
As we enter this holy vocation of marriage,
we do so in order to respond more deeply
to the call you have given us in baptism
to pursue the fullness of holiness, the perfection of love.
We commit ourselves to promote
in our marriage and in our family
your kingdom of truth and love,
justice and peacemaking,
compassion and forgiveness.
We dedicate ourselves more intensely
to the service of one another, of our family

and of the wider community of humankind
in this broken and sin-torn world.
In this Spirit, O Lord,
we now proclaim our marriage vows.
I, N., give myself to you, N., as your wife/husband,
and accept you as my spouse in a bond of love, respect and caring
until the completion of our earthly journey together.
I commit myself to live our marriage
as a sacrament of Christ's presence and love in our lives,
so that we may grow in holiness,
and be a blessing to our family
and to all those whose lives we touch.

The couple would do best to pronounce their commitment facing each other with the use of a microphone, so as to be heard easily by the entire congregation.

Hopefully, these suggestions might inspire individual couples to create their own formula for their wedding ceremony (or anniversary celebration), in ways that will reflect the fuller meaning of Christian marriage as rooted in the baptismal commitment.

part three

Marriage: A Life of Prayer

*T*oo often we may think of prayer as our trying to change God. Rather, prayer is important because it opens us consciously to God who has the power to bring about radical change in us.

Six days later, Jesus took with him Peter and James and his brother John and led them up a high mountain, by themselves. And he was transfigured before them, and his face shone like the sun, and his clothes became dazzling white. Suddenly there appeared to them Moses and Elijah, talking with him. Then Peter said to Jesus, "Lord, it is good for us to be here; if you wish, I will make three dwellings here, one for you, one for Moses, and one for Elijah." While he was still speaking, suddenly a bright cloud overshadowed them, and from the cloud a voice said, "This is my Son, the Beloved; with him I am well pleased; listen to him!" When the disciples heard this, they fell to the ground and were overcome by fear. But Jesus came and touched them, saying, "Get up and do not be afraid." And when they looked up, they saw no one except Jesus himself alone. (Matthew 17:1–8)

117

This narrative gives us a glimpse of how Jesus was transfigured in prayer (see also Luke 9:28–29), and how three disciples experienced this reality. Reflection on this text can also provide insight into the transforming power of prayer in our own lives.

In this book we have been reflecting on how our faith in Christ can enrich our experience of marriage. Such a faith experience obviously implies a prayer life. In this final section we explicitly reflect on the transforming power of prayer in our marital journey. We first treat prayer as a response to God's action in our lives. We then consider several basic forms of prayer as they especially apply to married life.

chapter twelve

PRAYER: A LIVING RESPONSE TO GOD

One older, traditional definition of prayer that many of us grew up with from earlier catechisms stated that prayer is "the raising of our minds and hearts to God." There is no error in this definition. Obviously, prayer involves the focusing of our consciousness and our love on God. What is inadequate about the definition is that it leaves out God's action in prayer. It can give the impression that prayer is something we initiate and wait for God to respond, whereas the reality is very much the reverse.

This chapter centers on two main theological insights regarding prayer. First, prayer is the human response to God who is already communicating to us.[1] Second, our prayer response is offered not only in those periods when we are formally and consciously "praying," but also in everything we do or say in answer to God's will. These two insights very much reflect the biblical narratives about the prayer experiences of three biblical people.[2]

It was God who took the initiative with Abraham and called him to leave his country, his kindred and his father's house "to the land that I will show you" (Genesis 12:1). Abraham's response was to leave and go forth as God had told him.

When the Israelites were enslaved in Egypt, it was not Moses who took the initiative and beseeched God to deliver the people. It was God who called him by name from the middle of the burning bush and made him aware of God's concern. God then gave the call to Moses: "So come, I will send you to Pharaoh to bring my people, the Israelites, out of Egypt" (Exodus 3:10). Moses' response to this prayer experience was to go and do what God had asked of him.

As we turn to the New Testament the same initiative of God is seen in the call of Mary to be the mother of Jesus. The angel Gabriel was sent by God to tell Mary that she was to bear a son and name him Jesus. Mary gave her verbal response: "Here am I, the servant of the Lord; let it be with me according to your word" (Luke 1:38). Then Mary lived that response as a faithful mother even unto Jesus' death on the cross (John 19:25).

Our treatment of prayer here will focus on how each of these experiences of prayer as a lived response to God's initiative has application to marriage as a life of prayer.

GO TO A LAND I WILL SHOW YOU

From the very beginning marriage is a journey into the unknown. We believe that this is what God is calling us to do. We have hopes and dreams, but no assurance of where it will lead. The shadow of so many unhappy marriages and of a high divorce rate looms overhead. If faith is a leap into the dark, a plunge into the unseen, then marriage is one of the biggest acts of faith we make. It involves belief in oneself, in the other and in the abiding presence and grace of God. So we hear the challenge, "Go to a land I will show you." In faith we utter our prayerful "yes," and go forth to live it.

This "yes," however, must be a *rational* act of faith, that is there must be clear reasons (from the Latin *ratio*) to believe we have the wherewithal to make it work. These reasons are not proofs or guarantees, for such do not exist in any act of faith. Rather they are built on clear indications in the dating relationship that there exists mutual responsibility, maturity, self-control, respect, sensitivity, generosity and love.

This is the opposite of an *irrational* leap into the dark, as occurs when one ignores signs of serious problems such as addictions, abuse, inability to communicate or self-absorption. It is always heart-rending when you try to point out such a problem to someone who is "in love," and get a response similar to the following examples. "It's true he has shoved me around and slapped me a few times," the young lady confided, "but he promised he would never do that after we got married." A young man once mentioned, "my fiancée has a serious drinking problem, but we love each other very much, and love can conquer all." "He has cheated on me a few times while we dated," another woman said, "but I believe the grace of the sacrament of matrimony will change that."

One of the most important purposes of marriage preparation is that the engaged and the persons counseling them read carefully and take seriously the signs in the dating relationship. Yes, love and marriage can influence people for the better, but they are incapable of working magic. "A tiger cannot change its stripes, a leopard cannot change its spots," as the old saying goes. Yes, God's grace can transform those who are open to it, but "grace builds on nature," as an age-old theological axiom states. Jesus performed a miracle at the wedding feast of Cana, but there was water in the jars before he changed it into wine.

These insights into the nature of faith that is required as the couple embarks on the pilgrimage of marriage have application at all the cross points that are encountered as the journey evolves.

If we are called to be parents, disturbing questions can immediately confront us. "Do we really want to bring an innocent child into this dangerous world?" "Do we have the virtues necessary to be good parents?" "Will we always have the means to provide for the well-being of our children?"

There are no definite answers that can take our fears away. But we hear God's words, "Go to a land I will show you." In faith we utter our prayerful "yes," and go forth to live it.

As the marital journey continues, unexpected events cross our path: a seriously challenged child, loss of a job, foreclosure of a home, a life-threatening illness. "Where do we go from here?" "Why did God let this happen?" "Where is God in our dark hour?" But we hear God's words, "Go to a land I will show you." In faith we utter our prayerful "yes," and go forth to live it.

The years march on. The children leave home. Retirement sets in. "How will this change our lives?" "Will it alter our relationship?" "Do we sell our house and downsize?" "What does the future hold?" But we hear God's words, "Go to a land I will show you." In faith we utter our prayerful "yes," and go forth to live it.

Finally death takes one of us. We face life alone, as a widow or widower. "How can I make it now?" "What is there to live for?" "Will I be able to bear the void?" But God's words are heard, "Go to a land I will show you." In faith one utters the prayerful "yes," and goes forth to live it.

And what about our deceased spouses? They too heard the voice, as all of us someday will, "Come to a land I will show you," a land that no eye has seen, no ear has heard, no mind has understood. In faith they uttered the prayerful "yes," and went forth to live it.

Then the loved one left behind remembers with joyful sorrow and sorrowful joy these words once written:

I am standing on the seashore.

A ship spreads her white sails to the morning breeze and starts for the ocean. I stand watching her until she fades on the horizon, and someone at my side says, "She is gone."

Gone where? The loss of sight is in me, not in her. Just at the moment when someone says, "She is gone," there are others who are watching her coming. Other voices take up the glad shout, "Here she comes," and that is dying.[3]

DELIVER MY PEOPLE

The faith experience that God had delivered their ancestors from slavery in Egypt and brought them to the Promised Land gave the Israelites a deep belief that God would continue to be their savior, their liberator, their deliverer. Accordingly, the psalmist could exclaim:

I love you, O LORD, my strength.
The LORD is my rock, my fortress, and my deliverer,
    my God, my rock in whom I take refuge,
    my shield, and the horn of my salvation, my stronghold.
I call upon the LORD, who is worthy to be praised,
    so I shall be saved from my enemies. (Psalm 18:1–3)

The author of Psalm 40 could also declare:

As for me, I am poor and needy,
    but the Lord takes thought for me.
You are my help and my deliverer;
    do not delay, O my God. (v. 17)

Inspired by this same type of confidence, Psalm 23 proclaims:

Even though I walk through the darkest valley,
    I fear no evil;
for you are with me;
    your rod and your staff—
    they comfort me. (v. 4)

This assurance that God was their security led these people of faith to plead for protection in every threatening situation. Their prayer for deliverance serves as a model for our prayer as married couples and parents. We fear for ourselves and for the safety of our loved ones, and the more deeply we love, the more real and intense those fears can become. Foremost among these is the fear of violent attacks on the part of evildoers: rape, abduction, spiritual and physical assault, and murder itself. So with the psalmist we turn to God:

> Show your wonderful love,
>> you who deliver with your right arm
>> those who seek refuge from their foes.
> Keep me as the apple of your eye;
>> hide me in the shadow of your wings
>> from the violence of the wicked.
> (Psalm 17:7–9, NAB)

We turn this prayer into action by creating in our homes a safe environment free from abuse and filled with personal concern and care. We live this prayer by keeping a watchful eye and shielding each other in the shadow of our protective presence.

We fear our own dark side, our proclivity toward evil, our personal sinfulness. With the psalmist, then, we pray:

> Deliver me from all my transgressions.
> Do not make me the scorn of the fool. (Psalm 39:8)

> O God, you know my folly;
>> the wrongs I have done are not hidden from you.
> …
> …rescue me
> from sinking in the mire;
> let me be delivered from my enemies
>> and from the deep waters.

Do not let the flood sweep over me,
   or the deep swallow me up,
   or the Pit close its mouth over me. (Psalm 69:5, 14–15)

We translate into our lives our verbal prayer for deliverance from sin by coming to grips with that within us that keeps us from closer union with God, our spouse and our family. We fulfill our prayer by being open to God's grace empowering us to avoid evil actions and to do good.

We realize too that our family exists in the context of the wider human community. Thus what harms anyone anywhere has an effect on all of us. With the psalmist we reach out beyond the confines of our own household and pray for those burdened with life's misfortunes:

Give justice to the weak and the orphan;
   maintain the right of the lowly and the destitute.
Rescue the weak and the needy;
   deliver them from the hand of the wicked. (Psalm 82:3–4)

Do not surrender your turtledove to the beast;
do not forget for ever the life of your oppressed people.
…
Do not let the downtrodden retreat in confusion,
give the poor and needy cause to praise your name.
(Psalm 74:19, 21, NJB)

In this twenty-first century we are overwhelmed by the individual and institutionalized injustices that continue to crush the poor, the homeless, the abused, the imprisoned and the victims of strife and war. We live out our verbal prayer for them not only by acts of charity to alleviate their suffering, but also by becoming involved in the struggle to change the societal structures that violate human rights and oppress the disadvantaged.

The God of deliverance to whom the psalmist prayed became fully revealed in Jesus. He himself prayed the prayer he taught us, "deliver us from the evil one" (Matthew 6:13, NAB). He put this prayer into action by delivering people from blindness, deafness and ills of every kind. He fulfilled this prayer by freeing people from evil spirits and forgiving their sins.

Jesus' determination to deliver from evil is highly symbolized in two events on the waters. In one he was asleep in the boat. "Suddenly a storm broke over the lake, so violent that the boat was being swamped by the waves." The disciples woke him: "Save us, Lord, we are lost!" He stood up, "rebuked the winds and the sea; and there was a great calm" (Matthew 8:23–27, NJB).

On another occasion when the disciples were far out on the lake, battling with a headwind and a heavy sea, Jesus came toward them, walking on the water. Peter said, "If it is you, command me to come to you on the water." When Jesus invited him to come, Peter got out of the boat and walked on the water toward Jesus. Peter did fine until he became frightened, and then he began to sink. Jesus at once put out his hand and held him up (Matthew 14:22–33).

On the night before he died Jesus repeated his prayer that his disciples be delivered from evil. "I am not asking you to take them out of the world, but to protect them from the evil one" (John 17:15). The next day he gave up his life for the fulfillment of this prayer. He died and passed into risen life that he might give us the Spirit to deliver us from our darkness and bring us to new light. In what has come down to us as the "Lord's Prayer" we are invited to pray with Christ, "deliver us from evil." We accept this invitation countless times in our private and communal prayers, and every time we celebrate the Eucharist or recite the rosary.

However, if we are really serious about this prayer, then we have to put it into action as Jesus did. Every time we say or do something to prevent a bad thing from happening to our spouse, our children and others, that effort becomes part of our prayer that God deliver us from evil. Whenever we help someone through a bad situation this becomes a living prayer for deliverance. It is a prayer in action when we nurse a family member who is ill, or help calm the emotional and spiritual storm in a heartbroken teenage child, or put out our hand to hold up an aging parent sinking into depression.

We also live this prayer for deliverance each time we open ourselves to the Spirit of God whom the Father and the risen Christ breathe upon us. In doing so we welcome the Spirit of Truth to dispel our ignorance, our disbelief, our proclivity toward deception in order that we might relate more humbly and honestly with our spouse and family. We allow the Spirit of Hope to drive out our fears and suspicions so that we may bond more intimately with one another. We invite the Spirit of Love to free us from apathy and self-centeredness and enkindle in us the fire of Divine Love.

BE IT DONE ACCORDING TO YOUR WORD

"Not everyone who says to me, 'Lord, Lord,' will enter the kingdom of heaven, but only the one who does the will of my Father in heaven" (Matthew 7:21). Mary is hailed in popular devotion for being the mother of Christ. But according to Jesus' own testimony, the real greatness of Mary resides not in the mere fact of her physical motherhood, but in her response to the will of God. When a woman called out from the crowd, "Blessed is the womb that bore you and the breasts that nursed you," he said, "Blessed rather are those who hear the word of God and obey it!" (Luke 11:27–28). On another occasion when he was told, "Your mother and your brothers are standing outside, wanting to see you," he responded, "My mother and my brothers are those who hear the word of God and do it" (Luke 8:20–21).

When Mary perceived the will of God at the Annunciation, she gave her verbal assent. She then went forth and translated her verbal "yes" into action. Her entire subsequent life as wife to Joseph and mother of Jesus became a prayer of response to the call of God.

There has been a tendency to idealize Mary's life as spouse and parent, and disassociate it from the actual historical context in which she lived in first-century Palestine. So often Mary is placed on a pedestal, and treated as though she floated above the ordinary circumstances of married life and was left untouched by the challenges of the world around her. Such a tendency does a serious disservice to Mary. It gives the impression that her "yes" to the will of God was relatively trouble-free and costless. It also renders Mary quite irrelevant to the struggles of the community of married Christians for whom she should be the model disciple of Christ.

Contemporary biblical and historical scholarship has shed a more realistic light on the actual political, cultural, economic and religious circumstances that surrounded Mary's earthly life. Some of these have been treated in chapter three in regard to the world in which Jesus lived. Here we wish to reflect on some of the aspects of that world as they specifically related to Jewish Palestinian women of that era.[4]

Elizabeth Johnson situates Mary in her sociological environment with this summary: "As a rural Galilean Jewish woman, known in the social roles of virginal girl, married wife, hard-working nurturing mother, and older widow, Miriam of Nazareth was also shaped by her society's laws, customs, and expectations regarding the respective roles of women and men."[5] Johnson then points out that the culture shaped by those laws and customs was patriarchal, and the majority of women were legally disadvantaged and powerless.[6]

The marriages of young people were arranged by their families. Mary would probably have been twelve or thirteen when she was betrothed.[7] After a year of betrothal she was transferred into Joseph's household and would have most likely become part of an extended family. Households ordinarily consisted of multigenerational groups of persons linked by marriage and descent.

Calling to mind the typical domestic architecture of Galilean villages, we can envision one or more extended families sharing a compound with common walls, courtyard workspaces, water cisterns, ovens, and rooftop areas. They would lend tools, utensils, and food materials back and forth. . . In this setting the segregation and seclusion of women, typical of higher-status families, was hardly possible. Nor did the family homestead function as a private space for living distinct from the public sphere of work. Rather, the family was a working group and its domicile a nexus of social and economic relations. Lack of privacy was a constituent feature of life. Miriam hardly had a room of her own.[8]

The traditional art that depicts the "holy family" as consisting of only Jesus, Mary and Joseph is challenged by the Gospel narratives themselves. Reference is made to the four brothers of Jesus, James, Joseph, Simon and Judas, and an unspecified number of sisters (Matthew 13:55–56, Mark 6:3). Through the centuries, three positions have been offered to explain how these "brothers and sisters" were related to Jesus: (1) they are the children of Mary and Joseph, born after Jesus' birth; (2) they are Joseph's children by a previous marriage; (3) they are Jesus' cousins.[9] This is not the place to go into the arguments offered for and against each of these positions. What is relevant here is that Mary did not live her prayerful, holy life fulfilling the will of God in a convent-like atmosphere nor in a quiet three-member nuclear family environment. Rather, regardless of which interpretation one accepts, the reality of these "brothers and sisters" means:

> that during her own adulthood Mary engaged in a great deal of direct or indirect parenting of a large brood. Along with the physical labor involved, this entailed all the reserves of energy and intelligence required in good child-rearing. When these other children are taken into account, the romanticized picture of an ideal "holy

family" composed of an old man, a young woman, and one perfect child does not hold up. There is a lot of noise, a lot of mess, a lot of work, a lot of conversation, perhaps a lot of laughter.[10]

The workload of a mother in such an extended family embraced a wide variety of tasks that went far beyond the teaching, training and caring for children. Providing food was a major factor in her daily schedule. She would care for the kitchen garden that supplied vegetables, and for the small animals like sheep, goats and perhaps some cows that "provided dairy products, occasional meat, and skins and wool for making clothing."[11] The processing and preserving of food involved threshing, drying, pounding and pitting of foodstuffs. The making and providing of clothing for the household entailed spinning, weaving and sewing garments.[12]

Obviously this is but a partial picture of the daily life of Mary. However, picturing her in the actual circumstances of her rural, peasant life sheds light on what it meant for her to give her prayerful yes to God amid the nitty-gritty of everyday life. It also relates Mary to the vast majority of married couples and parents today who live out, in the routine of their daily lives, the verbal "yes" they gave to God and to one another when they pronounced their wedding vows. Our daily prayer, "your will be done on earth as it is in heaven" is written into the marrow of our married lives with every action, however sublime or mundane, that is done in answer to what we perceive as God's will for us at any given moment. All we do as a married couple—from making love, rearing the children and providing a livelihood, to cleaning, doing laundry and preparing meals—can become a living prayer of the offering of ourselves in response to the God who continually calls us in Christ Jesus by the power of the Spirit.

It was God who took the initiative in the religious experience of Abraham, Moses and Mary of Nazareth. Under the impact of God's grace they responded. Abraham went to the land God would show him. Moses became the one through whom God would deliver the

Israelites from slavery in Egypt and lead them to the promised land. Mary gave her "yes" and brought Jesus into the world.

These experiences tell us something about the meaning of prayer in our own married lives.

All of our prayer is in response to God who first communicates to us. In every stage of the marital journey a new challenge appears. God calls us to go forward to "a land I will show you." Putting aside our fears we pray our "yes," and put it into action by going forth in faith and trust to pursue the next stage of the journey, wherever that may lead. Throughout our marriage and parenting God calls us to be channels of his deliverance from evil of ourselves, our spouse and our children. We give our prayerful "yes," and put it into action with every effort we make to prevent harm and injury, and to provide safe harboring. We are called like Mary to live our married lives according to God's word. We give our verbal response, "your will be done on earth as it is in heaven," and put it into action by becoming the best spouse and parent we are called to be.

Concluding Prayer
O Loving God, we thank you
for communicating yourself to us in prayer.

It was in prayer that you encountered Abraham
and sent him to a land he had never seen.
Lord, at every new stage of our marital journey
you invite us to new horizons we have not yet envisioned.
Give us the faith and the courage
to follow your call wherever it leads.

It was in prayer, O God,
that you revealed yourself to Moses in the burning bush
and commissioned him to deliver your people from slavery.
Give us, Lord, the wisdom and the compassion

to protect from all harm
those whom you have entrusted to our care.

It was in prayer, O God,
that you called Mary to be the mother of Jesus.
She let it be done according to your word.
Help us, Lord, throughout our married life
to hear your word
and go forth and do it.
We pray this in the name
of Jesus, your Son, Amen.

FOR DISCUSSION

1. How do you experience prayer as your response to God who first communicates to you?
2. How has prayer enriched your marriage?
3. How do you see the lived prayer of Mary, as described in this chapter, relating to your own marital situation?

chapter thirteen

PRAYING IN COUNTLESS WAYS

Rejoice always, pray without ceasing, give thanks in all
circumstances; for this is the will of God in Christ Jesus for you.

—1 Thessalonians 5:16–18[1]

*G*od is constantly communicating to us in a diversity of ways.
Hence, there are a variety of forms in which we give our response to
God both in verbal prayer and in our lived "yes" to God's will for us.
In this chapter we reflect on four of these: worship, thanksgiving,
petition and forgiveness, as they apply specifically to prayer in the
lives of married couples.

PRAYER OF WORSHIP

> Enter, let us bow down in worship;
>> let us kneel before the LORD who made us.
> For this is our God,
>> whose people we are,
> God's well-tended flock. (Psalm 95:6–7, NAB)

There are many aspects to the prayer of worship. Here we will focus
on five of them.

1. *To worship God is to acknowledge God as the Ultimate Transcendent One.* So while we believe that God is intimately with us and deeply connected to us, we humbly admit that God is totally beyond our comprehension. While in one way we know the God who communicates to us in the depths of our being, we realize there is infinitely more to this God that we cannot begin to understand. We bow down to the Unknowable God who touches us at the core of our existence.

Consequently, we avoid the temptation to make God according to our own image and likeness. Instead we try to discover how we can grow in God's own image.

When we speak *of* God, we are conscious that everything we say is by imperfect comparison to the human situation and therefore profoundly inadequate.

In humble awe of the Transcendent One we also avoid speaking *for* God, as if anyone can perfectly read God's "mind." We refuse to entertain the mentality that identifies God's will for another person with what I want that person to do, or that analyzes with "certitude" God's "reasons" why things happen as they do. We avoid such statements as: "God allowed this tragedy as a punishment for such and such a sinful action"; "God had a good purpose for having your husband die of a heart attack at a young age and leaving you with four young children."[2] How does anyone know?

What we do know in faith is that whatever happens God is with us, and so we bow down in worship to God who is our rock, our comforter, our healer, our salvation. We contemplatively bask in the awesome and intimate presence of our infinitely loving God who wills to carry us through even the darkest hours.

2. *We worship God as our Creator.* We acknowledge God as the One upon whom we are totally dependent for all we are, all we have and all we do. Hence, we do not take personal credit for our gifts and accomplishments. Nor do we think ourselves superior as human

beings to our spouse, our children or others who are different from us. We realize our responsibility and accountability to God for all the gifts God has bestowed upon us. In worship we offer back to God what God has gratuitously given to us.

3. *We worship God as the Designer of marriage and sexuality.* Accordingly, we appreciate our marital state and our sexual intimacy as a call from God and a way to God. We treat each other in the dynamics of our relationship as God would have us do. In that context we acknowledge our spouse, our marital companionship and sexual intimacy as gifts from God, and treat them as such.

4. *We worship God as the ultimate Creator of our children.* We do not own them. They are the possession of God. We are not the ultimate givers of their life. We are the channels through whom God enlivens them. We are responsible to God for how we parent them.

The Lebanese poet Kahlil Gibran expresses this well:

Your children are not your children.
They are the sons and daughters of Life's longing for itself.
They come through you but not from you,
And though they are with you, yet they belong not to you.
You may give them your love but not your thoughts.
For they have their own thoughts.
You may house their bodies but not their souls,
For their souls dwell in the house of tomorrow, which you cannot
    visit, not even in your dreams.
You may strive to be like them, but seek not to make them like you.
For life goes not backward nor tarries with yesterday.
You are the bows from which your children as living arrows are sent
    forth.
The archer sees the mark upon the path of the infinite, and He
    bends you with His might that His arrows may go swift and far.
Let your bending in the archer's hand be for gladness;

For even as he loves the arrow that flies, so He loves also the bow that is stable.[3]

5. *We worship God in God's presence in each other.* We believe that God dwells in us, and we acknowledge that faith awareness by the reverence, respect, care, love and spirit of service with which we treat our spouse, our children, and all those whom we encounter. In offering the gift of ourselves to each other we are offering the gift of ourselves to God.

PRAYER OF THANKSGIVING

The realization of our total dependence on God leads us to gratitude for all who God is for us, and for all God does for us and gives to us. We show this appreciation, as the psalmist does; first in word:

> We give thanks to you, God, we give thanks to you,
> as we call upon your name, as we recount your wonders.
> (Psalm 75:1, NJB)

And then in song:

> O give thanks to the LORD, call on his name;
> make known his deeds among the peoples.
> Sing to him, sing praises to him;
> tell of all his wonderful works.
> Glory in his holy name;
> let the hearts of those who seek the LORD rejoice.
> (Psalm 105:1–3)

Some of these wondrous deeds are spelled out in Psalm 136: the creation of the heavens, the earth and the waters, the sun to rule the day and the moon and stars to rule the night; the saving of the Israelite people from slavery in Egypt; and providing food for all living creatures. What is gratefully celebrated beyond all the works and wonders of God is God's faithful and enduring love:

It is good to give thanks to the LORD,
  to sing praises to your name, O Most High;
to declare your steadfast love in the morning,
  and your faithfulness by night,
to the music of the lute and the harp,
  to the melody of the lyre. (Psalm 92:1–3)

Appreciation for what God has done in general becomes quite personal as we reflect on what God has done specifically for us in our own individual journey:

I give thanks to you, O Lord my God, with my whole heart,
  and I will glorify your name forever,
For great is your steadfast love toward me;
  you have delivered my soul from the depths of Sheol.
(Psalm 86:12–13)

For Christians our gratitude rises to new intensity for the gift of Jesus Christ and what he has meant for our salvation. With Paul we can apply to ourselves this prayer:

But, thanks be to God, who in Christ always leads us in triumphal procession, and through us spreads in every place the fragrance that comes from knowing him. (2 Corinthians 2:14)

And with Paul we can give special thanks for Jesus' conquering of sin and death:

"Death has been swallowed up in victory."
"Where, O death, is your victory?
  Where, O death, is your sting?"
The sting of death is sin, and the power of sin is the law. But thanks be to our God, who gives us the victory through our Lord Jesus Christ. (1 Corinthians 15:54–57)

As we reflect on these gifts and all the gifts that come to us each day in our individual lives, and in our marriage, our sexual intimacy and our parenting, we ask the question raised by the psalmist, "What shall I return to the LORD / for all his bounty to me (Psalm 116:12)?" One answer to this question is suggested in Jesus' parable of the talents (Matthew 25:14–30). We show our appreciation to God by taking all the gifts God has given us and utilizing them to the fullest for our own growth in personal integrity and for the well-being of others.

On a final note, most of God's blessings come to us mediated through other people, especially our parents, our spouses and our children. Our thanks to God ought to include gratitude to all those who have been channels of God's graces to us.

PRAYER OF PETITION

Three of the major petitions that Jesus instructs us to ask for are the gift of the Holy Spirit, God's kingdom and righteousness, and our daily bread. We reflect on the significance each of these petitions has for the prayer life of married couples and their families.

Praying for the Spirit

> So I say to you, Ask, and it will be given you; search, and you will find; knock, and the door will be opened for you. For everyone who asks receives, and everyone who searches finds, and for everyone who knocks, the door will be opened. Is there anyone among you who, if your child asks for a fish, will give a snake instead of a fish? Or if the child asks for an egg, will give a scorpion? If you then, who are evil, know how to give good gifts to your children, how much more will the heavenly Father give the Holy Spirit to those who ask him! (Luke 11:9–13)

Matthew's version of this saying reads, "How much more will your Father in heaven give good things to those who ask him" (7:11). I like the connection between Matthew's "good things" and Luke's "gift of the Spirit," for God's Spirit is the source of the most important gifts that make a real difference in our lives. If we are open to God's Spirit not only do many "good things" flow from that, but we also have the light, the strength and the courage to deal constructively with the "bad things" that inevitably come our way.

On a personal note, the older I have gotten, and the longer I have been a spouse, a parent and a grandparent, the more I have found myself praying first and foremost for the Holy Spirit to breathe deeply upon me and my loved ones. For in praying for the Holy Spirit we are opening ourselves to what traditional church teaching has identified as the seven gifts of the Holy Spirit: wisdom, understanding, counsel, fortitude, knowledge, piety and fear of the Lord; and the twelve fruits of the Spirit: charity, joy, peace, patience, kindness, goodness, generosity, gentleness, faithfulness, modesty, self-control and chastity. It takes little imagination to see how directly these gifts and fruits of the Spirit influence and enrich the quality of our spousal and family relationships.

We pray to the Spirit for knowledge, understanding, wisdom and counsel in our lives, our marriage and our parenting. We ask for knowledge to allow us to escape our narrow-mindedness, broaden our horizons, enrich our lives, and be in touch with reality. We beseech the Spirit for understanding so that we can perceive correctly where the other is coming from, what the other means by what he or she says and does, and thus harmoniously accept our differences and confirm the similarities that bind us together. We bare ourselves open to the Spirit of wisdom that we might have insight that enables us to discern the inner qualities of each other and the under-the-surface dynamics of our relationships, thus empowering us to make correct judgments and decisions. We go to the Spirit for counsel and guidance as we wend our way through the maze of situations and circumstances that touch our family life.

We also ask God to imbue us with the Spirit that we might grow in piety because our devotion to God enhances our devotion to one another; and that we might have fear of the Lord, in the biblical sense of a readiness to do God's will.[4]

We pray deeply for the Spirit to endow us and our family with charity, joy, peace, patience, gentleness, kindness, generosity and faithfulness because the life-giving and nurturing qualities of our marriage and parenting are directly built on these fruits of the Spirit.

In opening ourselves to the Spirit we grow in modesty, self-control and chastity that are integral to a life of sexual intimacy that truly nourishes not only the physical but also the emotional and spiritual dimensions of our marital union.

In brief, when Jesus promises that God will give the Spirit to anyone who asks, we have the assurance of all the essential gifts necessary to achieve a blessed and happy marriage, regardless of whatever trials and difficulties may beset us. If we have the Spirit, we truly possess the "good things" that make the real difference in our life journey.

Seeking God's Kingdom

> But strive first for the kingdom of God and his righteousness, and
> all these things will be given to you as well. (Matthew 6:33)

There is an intrinsic connection between praying for the gift of the Spirit and seeking God's kingdom. To seek God's kingdom is to allow God to reign in our lives. Put another way, it is to let God influence the way we speak, act and treat others. This, of course, can only be done with the grace of the Holy Spirit.

In two earlier chapters we have treated certain aspects of the kingdom of God as they relate to marital spirituality. Here we recall the qualities of the kingdom of God that are mentioned in the preface to the eucharistic prayer for the feast of Christ the King:

> As king he claims dominion over all creation,
> that he may present to you his almighty Father,

an eternal and universal kingdom:
a kingdom of truth and life,
a kingdom of holiness and grace,
a kingdom of justice, love and peace.[5]

It is quite evident that if we seek in prayer and in action to enrich our marriage and our family life with these seven characteristics, then everything that is necessary for true happiness will follow. For these are indeed the very realities that spell the difference between relationships that are mutually fulfilling and joyful and those that are not.[6]

Our Daily Bread

Give us this day our daily bread. (Matthew 6:11)

Jesus has us pray with him for our daily bread. He translated that verbal prayer into prayerful action. He fed a crowd of thousands through the multiplication of the loaves and fishes. He felt sorry for the people and did not want to send them away hungry lest they "faint on the way" (Matthew 15:32–38). After his resurrection Christ provided a miraculous catch of fish for his apostles who had been out all night and caught nothing. He then had breakfast for them on the shore (John 21:1–14).

The concern that Jesus has for our daily bread goes far beyond the physical. He wants us to have the bread that nourishes the spiritual dimension of our being. "Do not work for the food that perishes, but for the food that endures for eternal life, which the Son of Man will give you. For it is on him that God the Father has set his seal" (John 6:27). He identifies himself as that bread, for he is the very Word of God: "I am the bread of life. Whoever comes to me will never be hungry, and whoever believes in me will never be thirsty" (John 6:35). As the risen Lord he continues to give of himself as our bread in Eucharist: "I am the living bread that came down from heaven. Whoever eats of this bread will live forever; and the bread that I will give for the life of the world is my flesh" (John 6:51).

We put our prayer for daily bread into action by seeking this bread on every level: not just the material bread, but also the bread of God's word, and the bread of Christ's risen body in Eucharist.

We work for the fulfillment of this prayer in visible, concrete ways every time we provide food for our family, the needy in our neighborhood and those starving throughout the world. We make this prayer come alive when we share with each other the bread of our word: our word of faith, our word of hope, our word of commitment and love, our word of personal, life-giving presence to one another.

"Give us this day our daily bread." We make it happen when we become the bread through whom God nourishes God's daughters and sons.

PRAYER OF FORGIVENESS

And forgive us our sins,
>   for we ourselves forgive everyone indebted to us. (Luke 11:4)

For if you forgive others their trespasses, your heavenly Father will also forgive you; but if you do not forgive others, neither will your Father forgive your trespasses. (Matthew 6:14–15)

One of our basic religious beliefs is that we are redeemed sinners. We are graced and called by God to live in loving union with God and one another. But none of us is perfect and we are all guilty of wrongdoing. No matter how hard we try, we at times fail and never perfectly come up to the standards we strive for. So in the penitential rite at the beginning of the Eucharist we humbly confess to God as well as to our sisters and brothers that we have sinned through our own fault, in our thoughts and in our words, in what we have done and in what we have failed to do.

This liturgical ritual, however, should be a public celebration of the private acts of forgiveness and sorrow expressed among individuals whenever their failures or actions have hurt others. Since the primary place where so many of our failings and offenses occur is in the home, saying, "I am sorry," and, "you are forgiven," ought to be a regular part of family life. Then we go to the church and publicly affirm the contrition and forgiveness we have already celebrated within our household.

There is a difference between forgiveness and reconciliation. To forgive means not to return evil for evil, to wish the person well, to pray for the person. To be reconciled means that friendship and harmony have been restored. It takes one to forgive, but two to be reconciled. I can control whether or not I forgive. I cannot alone control whether or not reconciliation will take place.

Jesus' teaching insists that we must forgive as God forgives. God is always forgiving, and so must we be, even if the other admits no wrong or rejects our forgiveness. Catholic tradition, however, has made clear that to be reconciled with God one must admit one's sin, be genuinely sorry for it, and be determined to try not to commit that fault again. The same conditions are necessary in order that reconciliation take place between two individuals.

Keeping the distinction between forgiveness and reconciliation in mind can help prevent the kind of anguish and guilt feelings I have sometimes heard expressed in counseling sessions. "I do not go to church any more," a middle-aged man admitted. "It would be hypocritical, because I am not a good Christian. I did not forgive my wife. I divorced her after putting up with four years of her marital infidelities. Had I been forgiving, I would have stayed with her." "I failed to be a forgiving parent," an aging widow tearfully complained. "I finally put my adult son out of the house, because I could no longer tolerate his frequent drunken rages." In both cases the person I counseled was totally forgiving and sympathetic. For reasons beyond their control, reconciliation was impossible. Their guilt feelings were rooted in their confusion of forgiveness with reconciliation.

There is an oft-heard maxim: "Forgive and forget." If all we mean by "forget" is that we let go of the offense, and don't use it to shame the person who has made a mistake, the axiom says something important. But if it is interpreted to mean that we can drive wrongs out of our minds entirely, we are asking for the impossible. Whatever happens to us, psychology maintains, is forever recorded either in our conscious or our unconscious. No offense can be obliterated. What we can and ought to strive to do is to remember it with a healed memory, that is, in a spirit of charity rather than with rancor or vindictiveness.

Concluding Prayer
O God, our Creator and Supreme Being,
we worship you and acknowledge you
as the One upon whom we depend
for all we are and all we have.

We give you thanks, O loving God,
for your faithful and lasting kindness
in giving us what we need
to sustain us on our lifelong journey.

With humility and gratitude we come before you
and plead for our daily bread,
especially the bread of your Word
and the bread of your personal presence.

Acknowledging our sinfulness
we pray for your forgiveness,
and commit ourselves to forgive one another
and to grow in union and peace.

In this spirit of worship and thanksgiving,
of humble seeking and forgiveness,
we offer to you in living prayer
our lives and our marital journey.

May they be ever enriched
by the grace of Jesus Christ
who lives and reigns with you
forever and ever. Amen.

FOR DISCUSSION

1. Of the four kinds of prayer described in this chapter, which is the one you find yourself most frequently praying? Why?
2. Which is the one you find yourself least frequently praying? Why?
3. Which of these four kinds do you share most easily and most frequently with your spouse and family? Why?

I am the light of the world. Whoever follows me will never walk in
darkness but will have the light of life.

—John 8:12

*J*esus, who changed the water into wine at the marriage
feast at Cana, is the light of the world who has conquered the darkness, has called us to be daughters and sons of the light, and has transformed the meaning of our lives and of our marriages. In turn, he has
given us the mission to be a light to others.

> You are the light of the world. A city built on a hill cannot be hid.
> No one after lighting a lamp puts it under the bushel basket, but on
> the lampstand, and it gives light to all in the house. In the same way,
> let your light shine before others, so that they may see your good
> works and give glory to your Father in heaven. (Matthew 5:14–16)

Married couples in our day live in a world plagued by many kinds of
darkness. This darkness inevitably overshadows our marital journey.
Are we to be overcome by it, or will we light the candle of our marriage and let it help dispel the gloom?

The spirituality of marriage described in this book suggests many ways in which, precisely through the quality of our marital union, we can help disperse the clouds that threaten society and family life today.

- Our deep respect for the rights of our partner can shine in the darkness of worldwide injustice.
- Our lived belief in the equality of the opposite gender can be a beacon that challenges the sexism that shadows our churches and our communities.
- Our peaceful approach to conflict resolution can shine as a counter to the violence and abuse that destroys life and ravages the human spirit.
- Our dedicated service to our spouse and our family can dispel the darkness of a culture that seeks to rule by lording it over others and depriving them of their freedom.
- The light of our lifelong marital faithfulness can challenge the disposability and lack of loyalty that marks so much of contemporary society.
- Our marital chastity, characterized by mutual respect for each other's sexuality, by permanent commitment, by care, sensitivity and responsibility for the other shines as a light against the darkness of casual, loveless sex and sexual exploitation of the vulnerable that plagues today's culture.

Over two and a half millennia ago the prophet Isaiah proclaimed:

Arise, shine, for your light has come,
  and the glory of the LORD has risen upon you.
For darkness shall cover the earth,
  and thick darkness the peoples;
but the LORD will arise upon you,
  and his glory will appear over you. (Isaiah 60:1–2)

A similar challenge is echoed in the First Letter of John:

> This is the message we have heard from him and proclaim to you, that God is light and in him there is no darkness at all. If we say that we have fellowship with him while we are walking in darkness, we lie and do not do what is true; but if we walk in the light as he himself is in the light, we have fellowship with one another, and the blood of Jesus his Son cleanses us from all sin. (1:5–7)

Our hope and our prayer is that we will be empowered to allow the risen Christ, the Morning Star, to be ever present in our marital journey, so as to help us be channels of his light and disband the shadows of the night! In this way may we work toward the ultimate fulfillment of that vision described in the book of Revelation:

> But the throne of God and of the Lamb will be in it, and his servants will worship him; they will see his face, and his name will be on their foreheads. And there will be no more night; they need no light of lamp or sun, for the Lord God will be their light, and they will reign forever and ever. (22:3–5)

.notes.

PART ONE

INTRODUCTION

1. Quotes throughout this section are taken from Raymond E. Brown, *The Anchor Bible*, vol. 29, *The Gospel according to John, I–XII* (Garden City, N.Y.: Doubleday, 1966), pp. 103–105.

CHAPTER ONE

1. See Dorothy M. Stewart, compiler, *The Westminster Collection of Christian Prayers* (Louisville, Ky.: Westminster John Knox, 2002), p. 339.

2. Some Johannine scholars see a double meaning here: Jesus expired, and in his death gives us the Spirit. The *New Jerusalem Bible* footnote on this verse puts it this way: "The last breath of Jesus is the first moment of the outpouring of the Spirit" (p. 1787).

3. *Webster's Ninth New Collegiate Dictionary* (Springfield, Mass.: Merriam-Webster, 1986), p. 268.

4. Gerald Foley, *Courage to Love... When Your Marriage Hurts* (Notre Dame, Ind.: Ave Maria, 1992), p. 67.

CHAPTER TWO

1. This connection between Trinitarian faith and Christian practice is brought out well in the title of Catherine Mowry LaCugna's monumental work, *God for Us: The Trinity and Christian Life* (New York: HarperCollins, 1991).

2. Segundo Galilea, *Spirituality of Hope* (Maryknoll, N.Y.: Orbis, 1988), p. 18.

3. *Lumen Gentium* (Dogmatic Constitution on the Church), 10–13.

CHAPTER THREE

1. John F. Clarkson, John H. Edwards, William J. Kelly, John J. Welch, trans., *The Church Teaches: Documents of the Church in English Translation* (St. Louis: B. Herder, 1955), p. 172.

2. See Raymond E. Brown, *The Birth of the Messiah* (New York: Doubleday, 1993), especially pp. 69–74; and Robert J. Hater, *The Catholic Family in a Changing World* (Orlando: Harcourt Religion, 2005), pp. 4–5.

3. For biblical sources and explanation of the limitations of Jesus' human knowledge see Raymond E. Brown, *Jesus God and Man* (Milwaukee: Bruce, 1967), especially chapter 2, "How Much Did Jesus Know?", pp. 39–102; Joseph A. Fitzmyer, *A Christological Catechism: New Testament Answers* (New York: Paulist, 1991), pp. 101–102; Richard P. McBrien, *Catholicism* (New York: HarperCollins, 1994), pp. 548–557.

4. McBrien, pp. 563–564 (emphasis original). See his whole section on the sexuality of Jesus, pp. 557–564.

5. For a good overview of the geographical, political and religious climate of Jesus' time, see Donald Senior, *Jesus: A Gospel Portrait* (New York: Paulist, 1992), especially chapter 2, "The World of Jesus," pp. 26–46. For insight about what it meant for Jesus to be from Galilee rather than Jerusalem, see Virgilio Elizondo, *Galilean Journey: The Mexican-American Promise* (Maryknoll, N.Y.: Orbis, 2000), especially pp. 50–56. An even more detailed picture of life in early first-century Galilee is found in Elizabeth A. Johnson, *Truly Our Sister: A Theology of Mary in the Communion of Saints* (New York: Continuum International, 2003), especially chapter 7, "Galilee: The Political-Economic World," pp. 137–161, and her treatment of the religious world in Galilee, pp. 166, ff. In this section I am primarily dependent on these three resources.

6. Senior, p. 27.

7. Elizondo, p. 51.

8. Elizondo, p. 51. The Spanish word *mestizaje* (from *mestizo,* "mixed," "hybrid") is used by Elizondo "to designate the origination of a new people from two ethnically disparate peoples" (p. 5).

9. Johnson, p. 141.

10. Johnson, p. 144.

11. Johnson, p. 144.

12. Johnson, p. 146.

13. Throughout this book I use the word *body* in the holistic sense of inspirited body, embodied spirit; *not* in the dualistic sense of body as opposed to spirit or soul.

14. This, of course, presupposes a mutually loving marriage where two equal partners regard each other with genuine respect, caring and sensitivity. God's love, respect and sensitive caring for us is mediated through the love, respect and caring we tender each other.

15. For example, one Catholic male student a few years ago proclaimed in class his confusion about the church's attitude toward marital intimacy. "On the one hand," he said, "the church holds that marital sexual intimacy is sacramental. On the other hand, anyone who wants to get married is automatically precluded from priestly ministry."

16. When we come to the topic of parenting in the marriage course, I ask the class for a raise of hands if they know any person their age who does not want children because of the violence in the world. Almost every hand goes up.

CHAPTER FOUR

1. The richness of this psalm is brought out in the commentary by Bertrand A. Buby, *With a Listening Heart: Biblical and Spiritual Reflections on the Psalms* (Staten Island, N.Y.: Alba House, 2005), pp. 138–139.

2. John Oxenham, quoted in *Soft as the Voice of an Angel,* (Fort Worth, Tex.: Brownlow, 1994), p. 1.

3. This kind of thinking reflects itself in the justification that some give today for mandatory priestly celibacy: "the priest should be celibate so that he can love God fully." Some might think this means that married love prevents one from fully loving God, which, of course, goes against the command of Jesus for all his disciples: "You shall love the Lord your God with all your heart, and with all your soul, and with all your strength, and with all your mind, and your neighbor as yourself" (Luke 10:27). It also stands in opposition to the church's teaching that marriage is a sacrament, an effective sign of Christ's grace and love. Marital love is not an obstacle to love of God, but an important means by which we can grow in that love.

4. Karl Rahner, *The Love of Jesus and the Love of Neighbor* (New York: Crossroad, 1983), p. 71.

5. This is found in *Magnificat*, vol. 5, no. 13, February, 2004, pp. 62–63. This is a wonderful monthly prayer book suitable for individual, couple and family prayer. It is biblically and liturgically oriented. It contains morning prayer, the order of the Mass and evening prayer for every day of the month. Their website is: www.magnificat.net.

CHAPTER FIVE

1. *The New Jerusalem Bible* (Garden City, N.Y.: Doubleday), p. 1613.

2. Raymond E. Brown, *The Gospel of St. John*, vol. 13, *New Testament Reading Guide* (Collegeville, Minn.: Liturgical, 1965), p. 67.

3. Raymond E. Brown, *The Gospel According to John XIII–XXI* (Garden City, N.Y.: Doubleday, 1977), p. 562.

4. This is brought out in Raymond Brown's two-volume work, *The Death of the Messiah* (New York: Doubleday, 1994). For the multiple references to the allusions the New Testament makes to the Suffering Servant in Isaiah see the index under "Isaiah, Suffering Servant" on p. 1565.

5. Pastoral Constitution on the Church in the Modern World (*Gaudium et Spes*), 48.

6. Anthony de Mello, *One Minute Wisdom* (New York: Doubleday, 1985), p. 171.

CHAPTER SIX

1. Unpublished prayer by Kathryn C. Roberts, 1992. It is quoted here with her kind permission.

CHAPTER SEVEN

1. From the *Roman Missal* (New York: Catholic Book Publishing, 1973).

PART TWO

INTRODUCTION

1. See "Christian Marriage: A Divine Calling," in *Marriage in the Catholic Tradition*, Todd A. Salzman, Thomas M. Kelly, John J. O'Keefe, editors (New York: Crossroad, 2004), pp. 98–108.

CHAPTER EIGHT

1. This comment particularly disturbs me because it ignores the fact that the majority of the poor do not have bootstraps with which to pull themselves up out of the condition of poverty. Indeed, many do not have boots, and some don't even have feet!

2. *Lives Together, Worlds Apart: Men and Women in a Time of Change: The State of World Population 2000* (UNFPA, United Nations Population Fund), p. 5.

3. *Lives Together*, p. 5.

4. *Lives Together*, p. 26.

5. These statistics appear with slight variance in every article I have seen on this topic.

6. I am using the word "rivalry" here in the sense of the first meaning that Webster's dictionary gives to the word "rival": "one of two or more striving to reach or obtain something that only one can possess," p. 1018.

CHAPTER NINE

1. Webster, p. 511.

2. I will be treating other aspects of this virtue in my reflection on prayer in part three.

3. *The New Jerome Biblical Commentary* (Englewood Cliffs, N.J.: Prentice Hall, 1990), p. 640.

CHAPTER TEN

1. The topic of prayer in marriage will be treated in much greater detail in part three of this book.

CHAPTER ELEVEN

1. This ritual is reprinted in *Magnificat,* vol. 7, no. 1, pp. 242–243.

2. These same questions are asked in the baptismal rites for adults and for

children. See *The Rites of the Catholic Church* (New York: Pueblo, 1983), pp. 98–99, 145–146, 206, 244–245.

3. *Rites of the Catholic Church*, pp. 561–562.

PART THREE

CHAPTER TWELVE

1. This definition served as the basis of my earlier book, *Teach Us to Pray* (Liguori, Mo.: Liguori, 1972). A similar approach to defining prayer is found in McBrien, p. 348.

2. See William P. Roberts, *Touchstones for Prayer* (Cincinnati: St. Anthony Messenger Press, 1983) for an extended treatment of God's initiative and the human response in the prayer of some key biblical figures.

3. Henry Scott Holland (1847–1918). This piece can be found under "Death" at www.prostatepointers.org/circle/holland.html.

4. In this section I am primarily indebted to Elizabeth Johnson's *Truly Our Sister*, especially chapter 9, pp. 185–206. A very fine, easy-to-read summary of recent scholarship regarding Mary's world is found in Robert P. Maloney, "The Historical Mary," *America*, vol. 193, no. 20, December 19–26, 2005, pp. 12–15.

5. Johnson, p. 185.

6. Johnson, p. 189.

7. Johnson, p. 190.

8. Johnson, p. 192.

9. Johnson, p. 195–198. See also Joseph A. Fitzmyer, *A Christological Catechism*, pp. 36–38.

10. Johnson, pp. 198–199.

11. Johnson, p. 200.

12. Johnson, pp. 200–202.

CHAPTER THIRTEEN

1. Silvio Fittipaldi's book, *How To Pray Always Without Always Praying* (Notre Dame, Ind.: Fides/Claretian, 1978) picks up on Paul's instruction to pray constantly. He reflects on prayer as questioning, as wonder, as

silence, as concentration, as relatedness, as perceptiveness, as grace and as wisdom.

2. I will never forget the night of my father's wake some fifty years ago. My mother, a very religious woman, came over to me and said: "If another person tells me it was God's will that my husband died of cancer, I am going to scream out loud."

3. Kahlil Gibran (1883–1931), *The Prophet* (New York: Alfred A. Knopf, 1966), pp. 18–19.

4. See McBrien, *Catholicism*, pp. 26, 208.

5. See, for example, *Magnificat*, vol. 7, no. 9, November, 2005, p. 281.

6. In *Marriage: Sacrament of Hope and Challenge* (Cincinnati: St. Anthony Messenger Press, 1988), pp. 53–56, I have explained in some detail the effect that these qualities of the kingdom of God can have on a marriage.

.index.

Abraham, 120, 130
à Kempis, Thomas, Saint, 48
Augustine, Saint, 12

baptism
  gift of the Holy Spirit in, 79
  of Jesus, 23–24
  meaning of, 79
  promises at, 109–110
  significance of, in marriage, 28
Bathsheba, 35
Brown, Raymond, 4–5, 55

Cana, wedding feast at. *See under*
  Jesus
celibacy, Catholic tradition and, 49
Chalcedon, Council of, 34
children
  concerns at having, 122
  God as creator of, 135
  religious education of, 104–105
Christ. *See* Jesus grace, 9–10
Claudel, Paul, 65
compassion
  forms of, 17
  of Jesus. *See under* Jesus
  lack of, 17
  in Scripture, 15
communion of saints, 71
conversion, 71
Courage to Love…When Your
  Marriage Hurts (Foley), 17–18

David, 35
death
  of Jesus. *See under* Jesus
DeGrazia, Ted, 84
de Mello, Anthony, 58

diaspora, Jewish, 15–16
diversity, 71

Easter, 25, 67, 109
Emerson, Ralph Waldo, 67
Eucharist, 26, 70, 100–102, 141
equality, between sexes, 82–84
  United Nations on, 82–83
Ezekiel, book of, 70

Foley, Gerald, 17
forgiveness, 142–144

Galilee
  accent of citizens, 37
  artisan class in, 38
  history of, 37
  significance of, 37
  society in, 38
generosity, 80–81
gentleness, 91–92
God
  acknowledgment of, 134
  as author of marriage, 99, 135
  as Creator, 134–135
  as deliverer, 126, 137
  as Father, 22–23
  as judge, 46
  incomprehensibility of, 46
  in Judeo–Christian tradition, 46
  kingdom of. *See under* Jesus. *See*
    also heaven
  as love, 45, 49
  as lawgiver, 46
  as model of marital love, 47
Golden Rule, 105

heaven, 71, 72

holiness
universal call to, 89–90
Holy Spirit, 21
communication of, 29
descent of,
on Jesus, 23–24
at Pentecost, 25, 30
disciples' experience of, 25
fruits of, 91
gifts of, 29–30, 139
help of, 24
praying for, 138
praying to, 139
promise of, 24, 140
humans
accepting limitations of, 40–41
conditioning of, 41
contingency of, 7
as image of God, 25
respect for, 27
sisters and brothers in Christ,
27–28
as temples of the Holy Spirit, 29

Incarnation
as fundamental Christian belief,
33
as God's self–communication, 33
Isaiah, book of, 54, 55, 148–149

Jerusalem, 37
Jesus
ancestry of, 34–35
authority of, 53, 56
baptism of, 23–24
brothers of, 129
charges against, 62
compassion of, 16, 17
culture of, 36–37
death of, 22, 36, 63

effect on marriage, 12
divinity of, 35
as face of God, 8
as Good Shepherd, 16
as high priest, 16–17, 38
humanity of, 34, 35–36
kingdom of, 70, 107
miracles of, x–ix, 3–4, 5, 6, 14, 16,
55
mission of, 97–98, 102
in others, 9
presence of, 8, 10–11
public ministry of, 10, 23, 55
as Redeemer, 28, 137
relationship with the Father, 22,
54
relationship with the Holy Spirit,
22
Resurrection of, 10, 63
service of, 53–56
sexuality of, 36
touch in ministry of, 14
as Word of God, 7–8, 10, 12, 18,
33–34
at wedding at Cana, x–ix, 3–4, 5, 6,
147
wounds of, 63
John, Gospel of, 4, 5, 8, 14, 62
Last Supper discourse, 21–22,
54–55
John the Baptist, Saint, 23–24, 36,
62
Johnson, Elizabeth, 128
Judah, 35
Judas, 62

Last Supper, 21–22. See also under
John, Gospel of
Lazarus, raising of, 16, 36
Lord's Prayer, the, 126

Los Niños, 84–85
love
  characteristics of, 50–51
  God as, 45, 49
  Luke, Gospel of, 90
  infancy narrative, 94
  Lumen Gentium, 89–90, 98, 99–100,
    102–103, 106

marital spirituality
  influence on wider culture, 148
  means of growth in, 9
marriage
  accepting spouse's flaws, 40
  baptism in, 28
  cultural support for, 42
  death of spouse, 122–123
  God's creative power in, 27, 100
  misunderstandings in, 64
  mutual love in, 48, 51
  partners as sinners, 28
  as path to sanctity, ix
  preparation for, 121
  present nature of, x
  relationship to culture, 42
  as sacrament, ix, 3, 18, 39, 77
  service in, 57–58
  sexuality in, 39–40, 49
  sharing moral and spiritual values
    in, 104
  as sign of Christ's love, x, 3, 18
  as vocation, ix, x, 77–78
Mary, 120
  Annunciation, 127
  betrothal of, 128
  cultural world of, 128
  earthly life of, 127–128, 130
  family of, 129
  as mother, 129–130
Matthew, Gospel of, 138

beatitudes, 90
genealogy, 34–35
Isaiah in, 91
McBrien, Richard, 36
mercy, 92–93
Moses, 15, 102, 120, 130–131
multiplication of loaves and fishes,
  16

Nazareth, 37–38
New Testament. *See* Scripture
Nicene Creed, 21
Nicodemus, 30

Old Testament. *See* Scripture

Patrick, Saint, 8
Paul, Saint, 9, 33–34, 50, 64, 91,
  100, 137
peacemaking, 93–95
Peter, Saint, 62, 64, 126
petition, 138–142
Pharisees, customs of, 5
poverty of spirit, 90–91
prayer
  as a couple, 100
  Jesus and, 118
  purpose of, 117
  trinitarian, 26
  See also forgiveness,thanksgiving,
    petition, worship
presence, 10–12
  God's touch in, 12
  longing for, 11–12
  recognizing in another, 26
  virtue in, 11
purity of heart, 93

Rahab, 35
Rahner, Karl, 50

retreats, in marriage, 104
Revelation, book of, 69–70
  marital imagery in, 73
Ruth, 35

sacraments. *See* baptism, Eucharist,
  marriage, wedding
sacrifice, 99–100
Sacrosanctum Concilium
  (Constitution on the Sacred
  Liturgy), 100–101
Scripture
  on compassion, 15
  on God's love, 46–47
  New Testament, 66, 120. *See also*
    specific books
  Old Testament, 22. *See also*
    specific books
  sharing, 12
Second Vatican Council
  on love, 50
  on marriage, x, 57
  on sacraments, 109
  understanding of grace, 9
selfishness, 80–81
  in U.S. culture, 81–82
Senior, Donald, 36–37
sexism, 72, 82–84
sexuality. *See under* marriage
Sign of Peace, 70
signs, definition of, 4
Solomon, 35
spouses. *See* marriage
Suffering Servant, 55–56
Synoptic Gospels, 5

Tamar, 35
thanksgiving, 136–138
Thomas, Saint, 64
touch
  Jesus' use of, 13–14
  kinds of, 14
  need for, in marriage, 15
Trinity
  in Gospel of John, 21–22
  Jesus as key to understanding, 22
  mystery of, 21
  understanding of, 21
Trinity Sunday, 21

Vatican II. *See* Second Vatican
  Council
violence
  effect on marriage, 41–42
  against women, 83–84
vows. *See under* wedding

wedding
  beginning of sacrifice at, 100–101
  symbolism of in Scripture, 5
  vows, 111–112
widow of Nain, 16
words
  as God's means of communication,
    13
  importance of, in marriage, 12–13
  Jesus as Word. *See under* Jesus
worship, 99, 133–136. *See also*
  prayer

.scripture index.

Old Testament

GENESIS
1:27	25
12:1	120
38	35

EXODUS
3:10	120
3:7–8	15

JOSHUA
2	35

Ruth
35	

2 SAMUEL
11	35

PSALMS
17:7–9	124
23:4	99
39:8	124
69:5, 14–15	124–125
74:19, 21	125
75:1	136
82:3–4	125
86:12–13	137
92:1–3	137
95:6–7	133
104:2, 5, 10, 19	46–47
104:24	47
105:1–3	136
116:12	138
120:1	92

ISAIAH
1:18	70
42:1	53
42:2–3	91
49:13–15	16

60:1–2	148
54:4–8	5

JEREMIAH
31:12	5

EZEKIEL
36:25–26	71

HOSEA
14:7	5

AMOS
9:13–14	5

ZEPHANIAH
3:17	85

New Testament

Matthew
1:1–16	24
1:23	7
3:16	24
3:17, 53	66
4:1–2	24
5:14–16	147
5:3–9	90
5:9	95
6:11	141
6:13	126
6:14–15	142
6:25–34	22
6:33	140
7:21	25, 127
8:14–15	14
8:23–27	126
9:35–36	16
12:19–20	91
13:55–56	129
14:22–23	126

15:32–38	141	2:14	94
17:1–8	117	2:34	94
18:23–35	92	2:52	35
20:25–28	53	23:34	10
22	69	23:46	10
23:13–36	94		
25:33–40	107	**JOHN**	
25:34	23	1:14	8
26:61	18	1:18	8
26:73	37	1:46	37
28:20	8	3:16	10
		6:27	141
MARK		6:35	141
2:19	5	6:51	141–142
6:3	129	8:12	147
8:2–3	16	9:6–7	14
10:13–16	14	11:32–35	16
		14:10	22
LUKE		14:11	22
1:35	23	14:16–17	24
1:38	120	14:18	8
3:22	29	14:2	23
4:14–15	24	14:24	22
4:18–19	24	14:25–26	24
5:12–13	14	14:9	8
6:36	15	16:12–14	25
6:46	25	16:15	22
7:11	138	16:28	22
7:36–50	14	17:15	126
8:20–21	127	17:21	30
8:43–48	14	17:3	12
9:28–29	118	19:25	120
11:27–28	127	2:1–11	3–4
11:4	142	2:19–22	18
11:9–13	138	20:19–23	10
12:6–7	23	20:19–23	25
15:11–32	23	21:1–14	141
15:4–7	23		
15:8–10	23	**ACTS**	
19:30	10	2:1–4	25
19:45–4	94	2:17–18	103

ROMANS
6:3–11   80
8:14–17   30
12:1–2   100

1 CORINTHIANS
7:8–9   78
12:12–31   27
12:12–31   84
13:4–7   50
15:54–57   137

2 CORINTHIANS
2:14   137
10:1   91

GALATIANS
3:28   84
5:22   29, 91

PHILIPPIANS
2:6–11   34

1 THESSALONIANS
5:16–18   133

HEBREWS
1:1–2   6
4:14–15   38
5:7–8   16

1 PETER
2:4–5, 9   98

1 JOHN
1:5–7   149
4:7–12, 30   45

REVELATION
9:10   103
19:5–8   70
21:1–4   73
22:3–5   149

CPSIA information can be obtained at www.ICGtesting.com
Printed in the USA
BVOW02s0015170215

387960BV00014B/167/P